Facets
of
the
Faith

Facets of the Faith

Everett L. Fullam

Chosen Books
Lincoln, Virginia 22078

The Practice of Evangelism by Canon Bryan Green; published by Charles Scribner, © 1951. Used by permission.

Poem by Harry Webb Farrington; from "The Hymnal of the Protestant Episcopal Church in the United States of America;" published by The Church Pension Fund, © 1940. Used by permission.

Facets of the Faith

Scripture quotations are from the Authorized Version of the King James Bible, Cambridge University Press, New Rochelle, N.Y.; the Jerusalem Bible, American Bible Society, New York, N.Y.; or the New English Bible, Oxford University Press, New York, N.Y. Some passages are paraphrased by the author.

Screwtape Letters by C. S. Lewis, copyright © 1959, Macmillan Publishing Company. Used by permission.

"May I commend to you once again Jesus Christ, the Prince of Peace, who has reconciled us to the Father through His death on the Cross, who seeks to be crowned the Lord of our lives, thus quieting the tempest in our hearts, and who seeks to create among men a fellowship of the redeemed who shall live to His glory forever and ever."

Father in Heaven, You have given us Your Holy Spirit as our teacher. Grant as we focus on facets of the faith that Your Word may be to us as bread to a hungry man, as a light upon our path, and as a swift sword in our hand, to the glory of Jesus, we pray. Amen.

CONTENTS

This book is taken from Father Fullam's talks broadcast on the Episcopal Series, March 28 to June 13, 1982.

PREFACE

Greetings in the Name of Jesus.

God has wrought a wonderful work in the pages of this book, and I am honored to be able to introduce it to you.

The twelve chapters which follow were prepared by Father Terry Fullam as talks for the Episcopal Series of the Protestant Hour produced by the Episcopal Radio-TV Foundation, Atlanta, Georgia. These chapters cover twelve facets of the Christian faith from a refreshingly clear and solid theological perspective, so that herein the reader will be exposed to the very essence of the Gospel. They are presented now in book form so that you may "read, mark, learn and inwardly digest" the rich material.

In an age of narcissism that has even given us an anthropocentric Gospel, Father Fullam herein directs our attention toward God: Father, Son and Holy Spirit. We are brought face to face with the varied facets of the Christian faith, which are presented so clearly by Father Fullam that we can see the Gospel shining forth in all its glory. In an age of confusion and doubt, these twelve chapters will point to the firm foundation that is God's Word to us, none other than Jesus the Christ, God Himself. In an age of searching, Father Fullam points us towards the answer, who is Jesus, the Son of God, and helps us to recapture that first love which is ours by faith.

This book then presents the eternal truth of the Gospel in terms that are clear, direct and profound. Father Fullam's talks are inspired and will inspire you.

I take great pleasure and thank God for being able to commend to you FACETS OF THE FAITH, which will help you to see and to proclaim Jesus, as God shapes you into a living stone, a facet of The Faith.

God bless you,

Theodore Baehr
President
The Episcopal Radio-TV Foundation, Inc.

I

Wanted: A Religion of the Heart

"And the Lord said unto Samuel, How long wilt thou mourn for Saul, seeing I have rejected him from reigning over Israel? Fill thine horn with oil, and go, I will send thee to Jesse the Bethlehemite: for I have provided me a king among his sons.

And Samuel said, How can I go? If Saul hear it, he will kill me. And the Lord said, Take an heifer with thee, and say, I am come to sacrifice to the Lord.

And call Jesse to the sacrifice, and I will shew thee what thou shalt do: and thou shalt anoint unto me him whom I name unto thee.

And Samuel did that which the Lord spake and came to Bethlehem. And the elders of the town trembled at his coming, and said, Comest thou peaceably?

And he said, Peaceably: I am come to sacrifice unto the Lord: sanctify yourselves, and come with me to the sacrifice. And he sanctified Jesse and his sons, and called them to the sacrifice.

And it came to pass, when they were come, that he looked on Eliab, and said, Surely the Lord's anointed is before him.

But the Lord said unto Samuel, Look not on his countenance, or on the height of his stature; because I have refused him: for the Lord seeth not as man seeth; for man looketh on the outward appearance, but the Lord looketh on the heart.

Then Jesse called Abinadab, and made him pass before Samuel. And he said, Neither hath the Lord chosen this.

Then Jesse made Shammah to pass by. And he said, Neither hath the Lord chosen this.

Again, Jesse made seven of his sons to pass before Samuel. And Samuel said unto Jesse, The Lord hath not chosen these.

And Samuel said unto Jesse, Are here all thy children? And he said, There remaineth yet the youngest, and, behold, he keepeth the sheep. And Samuel said unto Jesse, Send and fetch him: for we will not sit down till he come hither.

And he sent, and brought him in. Now he was ruddy, and withal of a beautiful countenance, and goodly to look to. And the Lord said, Arise, anoint him: for this is he.

Then Samuel took the horn of oil, and anointed him in the midst of his brethren: and the spirit of the Lord came upon David from that day forward. So Samuel rose up, and went to Ramah"   (I Samuel 16:1 - 13).

Some time ago I listened to a young seminarian, a candidate for the ministry, tell a group of clergy that he did not believe any of the teachings of the Christian Church. Yet week after week that young seminarian stands before a local congregation and leads them in the words of the creed: "I believe . . . ."

It reminded me of God's word to the prophet Isaiah:

"This people draw near with their mouth and honor me with their lips, while their hearts are

far from me, and their fear of me is a commandment of men learned by rote" (Isaiah 29:13).

It makes no difference to the Almighty whether someone is a parishioner in the pew, a singer in the choir or a
minister in the pulpit. God is not fooled by outward
appearances, for He views us from a divine perspective.

I know of no better illustration than in the Old Testament book of I Samuel, where we read the fascinating
story of the rise and fall of Saul, the first king of Israel. It is
a drama in two acts.

The first act opens with Samuel, the servant of the Lord,
anointing Saul as king. Saul's reign began with great
promise. He was able quickly to unite his people and defeat
their common foe. But his reign that began in promise
ended in defeat and despair. Little by little, Saul turned his
heart from the Lord and did that which was evil in His
sight. As a result, God rejected Saul as king over Israel, and
sent Samuel to bear the fateful message to the anointed
ruler:

"And Samuel said to Saul, 'You have done fool-
ishly; you have not kept the commandment of
the Lord your God, which he commanded you;
for now the Lord would have established your
kingdom over Israel forever. But now your kingdom shall not continue; the Lord has sought out
a man after his own heart; and the Lord has
appointed him to be prince over his people,
because you have not kept what the Lord commanded you'" (I Samuel 13:13-14).

The second act of this Old Testament drama begins with
Samuel mourning the downfall of Saul, until the word of
the Lord comes to him:

> "How long will you grieve over Saul, seeing I
> have rejected him from being king over Israel?
> Fill your horn with oil, and go; I will send you to
> Jesse the Bethlehemite, for I have provided for
> myself a king among his sons" (I Samuel 16:1).

So Samuel made his way to the little town of Bethlehem
in Judea, where he invited everyone—especially Jesse and
his sons—to a public sacrifice. As the sons of Jesse each
approached the altar with a sacrifice, Samuel wondered
which one the Lord had chosen to be king over Israel in the
place of Saul. All seven were strong and sturdy, and one
stood head and shoulders above the rest.

Eliab was a handsome man, powerful and ruggedly built.
His very bearing and stature commanded respect. As he
approached the altar, Samuel thought to himself, *Surely this
is the one.*

But at that moment, Samuel heard some remarkable
words from the Lord:

> "Do not look on his appearance or on the height of his
> stature, because I have rejected him; for the Lord sees
> not as man sees; man looks on the outward appear-
> ance, but the Lord looks on the heart" (I Samuel 16:7).

If I were to choose a single text for this chapter, I would
choose these words of the Lord God to Samuel:

> *"Man looks on the outward appearance, but the Lord looks
> on the heart."*

From a human point of view, Jesse's son Eliab possessed
all the qualifications of a king. He was tall, magnetic in
personality, fairly exuding those qualities of leadership
that made men rally around him. Physically, he was every
inch a king. Yet God passed him over in favor of his

younger brother David, whom Samuel anointed that day as king.

I can summarize my point very simply. The God with whom we have to do is a searcher of hearts; and what matters to Him is not what we look like on the outside, but what we are really like on the inside.

It was David, the youngest brother, the keeper of the sheep, whom God called "a man after my heart, who will do all my will" (Acts 13:22), and whom God chose to lead His people Israel. Years later, as an old man, David turned the kingdom over to his son with these words:

> "And you, Solomon my son, know the God of
> your father, and serve him with a whole heart
> and a willing mind; for the Lord searches all
> hearts, and understands every plan and thought"
> (I Chronicles 28:9).

Jesus made the same point in the New Testament. "All the churches shall know," He declared in Revelation 2:23, "that I am he who searches mind and heart." He meant, quite simply, that if our religion is to be accepted by Almighty God, it must be a religion of the heart, and no mere outward performance.

No one knows better than I, as a clergyman who grew up in a God-fearing home, how easy it is to come to church week after week and go through the motions of worshiping God: standing when we are supposed to stand, kneeling when we are supposed to kneel, reading the words that are set before us, and singing the hymns that are announced. We may then go home, congratulate ourselves for doing our duty toward God for another week, and proceed to forget all about Him.

Can we possibly believe God is fooled by this kind of charade? "For the Lord sees not as man sees; man looks on the outward appearance, but the Lord looks on the heart."

This was the very charade played out by the Pharisees, the religious "churchgoers" of Jesus' time. So far as men could tell, the Pharisees were very spiritual. They appeared to keep every detail of the Law. They prayed often in public places.

But God was not impressed. Do you recall Jesus' censure of them? "This people honors me with their lips," He exclaimed, quoting the passage from Isaiah 29, "but their heart is far from me" (Matthew 15:8). Another time He warned His disciples to "beware of the leaven of the Pharisees, which is hypocrisy" (Luke 12:1).

What is hypocrisy? Hypocrisy is looking one way on the outside, and being another way on the inside. Jesus reserved His most searing denunciation for the scribes and the Pharisees:

> "You are like whitewashed tombs, which out-
> wardly appear beautiful, but within they are full
> of dead men's bones and all uncleanness. So you
> also outwardly appear righteous to men, but
> within you are full of hypocrisy and iniquity"
> (Matthew 23:27-28).

In God's view, the attitude of the heart is all-important. So it is that the writer of the Proverbs cautioned us "to keep your heart with all vigilance; for from it flow the springs of life" (Proverbs 4:23). It is in the heart that faith and unbelief have their source.

The psalmist wrote,

> "The fool says in his heart, 'There is no God'"
> (Psalm 14:1).

And conversely, Paul wrote:

> "If you confess with your lips that Jesus is Lord

and believe in your heart that God raised him from the dead, you will be saved. For man believes with his heart and so is justified, and he confesses with his lips and so is saved" (Romans 10:9-10).

It is because God is interested in the heart that Jesus gave this warning:

"Beware of practicing your piety before men in order to be seen by them; for then you will have no reward from your Father who is in heaven. Thus, when you give alms, sound no trumpet before you, as the hypocrites do in the synagogues and in the streets, that they may be praised by men. Truly, I say to you, they have their reward. But when you give alms, do not let your left hand know what your right hand is doing; so that your alms may be in secret; and your Father who sees in secret will reward you. And when you pray, you must not be like the hypocrites; for they love to stand and pray in synagogues and at the street corners, that they may be seen by men. Truly, I say to you, they have their reward. But when you pray, go into your room and shut the door and pray to your Father who is in secret; and your Father who sees in secret will reward you" (Matthew 6:1-6).

It is because God is interested in the heart that Jesus said to those who criticized His disciples for eating with unwashed hands:

"Do you not see that whatever goes into the mouth passes into the stomach, and so passes

on? But what comes out of the mouth proceeds
from the heart, and this defiles a man. For out of
the heart come evil thoughts, murder, adultery,
fornication, theft, false witness, slander. These
are what defile a man; but to eat with unwashed
hands does not defile a man" (Matthew 15:17-
20).

This suggests what, to Jesus, constituted sin. He con-
ceived of sin, not so much a set of overt acts that a man
does, as the evil intentions within that man's heart.

The Law stated, "Thou shalt not kill," but Jesus taught
that if a man had hatred in his heart, it was as if, in the sight
of God, he had actually committed murder. The Law
stated, "Thou shalt not commit adultery", and there were
those who congratulated themselves on keeping this pre-
cept. But Jesus taught if a person so much as looks at
another with lust in his heart, it is as though, in God's
sight, he has committed adultery.

> *"For the Lord sees not as man sees; man looks on the outward
> appearance, but the Lord looks on the heart."*

Because God is interested in the heart, Jesus taught that
the Law is fulfilled perfectly when we love God with all our
heart, soul and mind, and our neighbors as ourselves (Matthew 22:37-40; Luke 10:27).

May I say that I am utterly convinced God is still interested in men, women and children whose hearts are right
in His sight? He is still interested in those who will pray, as
David of old prayed, "Create in me a clean heart, O Lord"
(Psalm 51:10).

I am convinced that the words spoken nearly three thousand years ago by the prophet Hanani to Asa, the king of
Judah, are just as true today as they were then:

"For the eyes of the Lord run to and fro throughout the whole earth, to show his might in behalf
of those whose heart is blameless toward him" (I
Chronicles 16:9).

Remember, God is not mocked. He cannot be duped. For
our God, as it says so beautifully in *The Book of Common
Prayer*, is a God "unto whom all hearts are open, all desires
known, and from whom no secrets are hid."

We pray, therefore: *Cleanse the thoughts of our hearts by the
inspiration of Your Holy Spirit, that we may perfectly love You, and
worthily magnify Your holy Name, through Christ our Lord. Amen.*

II

Into His Courts With Praise

"Praise ye the Lord. Praise God in his sanctuary: praise him in the firmament of his power.

Praise him for his mighty acts: praise him according to his excellent greatness.

Praise him with the sound of the trumpet: praise him with the psaltery and harp.

Praise him with the timbrel and dance: praise him with stringed instruments and organs.

Praise him upon the loud cymbals: praise him upon the high sounding cymbals.

Let everything that hath breath praise the Lord. Praise ye the Lord " (Psalm 150).

If a visitor from another planet came to earth and attended a service of Christian worship, it would not take him very long—nor would he have to be especially perceptive—to discover that the essence of Christian worship is praise.

Simply listening to the hymns that we sing—"Praise, My Soul, the King of Heaven," or "Praise to the Lord, the Almighty, the King of Creation," or "Praise God from whom all blessings flow; Praise Him, all creatures here below; Praise Him above, ye heavenly host; Praise Father, Son, and Holy Ghost"—would suggest to our visitor that Christians have been enjoined to praise the Lord, to bless Him, to exalt His holy Name.

Praise is so much a part of worship that the expression to "praise" God means much the same as to worship Him. And the word "praise" has become so much a part of our Christian vocabulary that we assume we know what it means.

I found my understanding seriously jogged, however, when a student of mine exclaimed in great impatience, "I could never worship a God who sits on a remote throne somewhere demanding the praise of His people! What kind of God is that?"

I had never thought of it like that. Is ours a God who sits on a remote throne somewhere demanding the praise of His people? Is He a God who has constantly to be told how wonderful He is?

We all know *people* like that—people who have to be reassured repeatedly of the beauty of their face, or the truth of their ideas, or the excellence of their virtue. Is our God like that? Is He like the wicked queen in *Snow White* who stands before the mirror and chants, "Mirror, mirror on the wall, who's the fairest of them all?" ("Oh, *You* are, Lord, You are.")

Is God like that? If He is, I think we should have nothing to do with Him.

Or perhaps you have noticed how, around every person of wealth and prominence, there seems to gather a group of people only too willing to lavish praise, just so as to extract some favor. Tell me, is the Church like that? Is the Church a group of people hovering over their God, lavishing praise upon Him, just so as to extract some favor from Him?

If that's what the Church is, who would want to be part of it?

The truth is, we will never understand praise so long as we think of it in terms of flattery. If to praise God means to flatter Him, we may never grasp why it is that over and over, especially in the Psalms, we are enjoined to praise our Maker.

But look at it this way. Have you noticed, when you have done something that filled you with intense delight, how natural it is to tell someone about it in enthusiastic terms? ("You ought to read that book; it's the best I ever read", or, "You should see that movie; I really enjoyed it.") You see, people instinctively praise whatever they enjoy. You don't have to tell a young man to praise the virtues of his girl-friend. I mean, that's doing what comes naturally!

There is a man in my congregation who loves to jog. Frankly, I cannot understand that sentiment. But he loves to get up a great while before dawn and run about town. And he commends it to everyone he meets with an evan-gelical zeal—not because he's a doctor (although he is), but because he actually enjoys it. People instinctively praise what they enjoy.

Further, have you noticed that, when enjoyment is shared, it is actually enhanced?

I have the opportunity through my ministry to travel widely throughout the world. Sometimes my wife goes with me, and sometimes she remains at home with our family. But she has a marvelous capacity to be able to enter into my joy. When I come back from a trip and relate some of the great blessings God bestowed on the ministry, Ruth is able to enjoy and enter into each one. And do you know what? It heightens my own experience of joy, because enjoyment shared is actually increased.

I think this provides a clue as to why, in our churches,

praise is so often self-conscious and unenthusiastic. Could it be there's not much enjoyment there? If praise is the spontaneous overflow of enjoyment, then I suspect true praise occurs only when people enjoy their God intensely.

This, for some, may seem a bit novel. We understand that we are to fear the Lord and hold Him in reverence and awe. But for many people, reverence means holding God at arm's length. The idea that we may enjoy the Lord has not taken hold in many of our churches.

But it is most Biblical! The Scripture tells us in numerous places that God delights Himself in us. (I cannot begin to understand why our God, who keeps the company of angels and archangels, would desire the fellowship of the like of you and me, but the Bible declares it is true.)

What's more, the Scripture tells us that God invites us to delight ourselves also in Him.

Think about it for a moment. If it's true that praise is a spontaneous overflow of enjoyment, isn't it also true that we need to enjoy our God intensely, to delight in His presence and in the fellowship of His people, in order for praise to erupt spontaneously from the center of our being?

The Presbyterians have a wonderful catechism. The first question of the catechism is, "What is the chief end of man?" And the answer is, "Man's chief end is to glorify God, and to enjoy him for ever."

I don't believe it could be put any better. That says the whole thing. To glorify God is always to enjoy Him, and to enjoy Him is always to glorify Him.

But let's consider the broader type of worship, of which praise is only a part. Three passages of Scripture in particular teach us important rules about worship.

The first passage is from the first chapter of Isaiah, in which the Lord, speaking of the worship of His people, says, "I hate your worship. I can't stand your singing. And your prayers make me sick." (It's a loose translation, I admit, but that's what it means!)

Why should the Lord be upset at the worship of His people? A few chapters later we find out:

> "This people draw near with their mouth and honor me with their lips, while their hearts are far from me" (Isaiah 29:13).

You see, God does not want lip service. Nothing is easier, as we saw in the last chapter, than to come into church, sit down, sing the hymns that are announced, read the Scripture lessons that are set before us, listen dutifully to the sermon, even receive the sacrament, and then go forth and imagine we've worshiped God. Is it as clear to you as it is to me that one can do all these things and not once worship the Lord?

The second passage of Scripture is from Matthew, in which the Pharisees complain to Jesus,

"Why do your disciples transgress the tradition of the elders? For they do not wash their hands when they eat" (Matthew 15:2).

Jesus answered their question with one of His own: "Why do you transgress the commandment of God," He returned, "for the sake of your traditions?"

To make sure they got the point, He cited a specific example—the fifth Commandment, which instructs us to honor our father and mother. For centuries, rabbinic tradition had interpreted that to include support for our parents in their old age, if necessary. But in the days of Jesus, the temple priests in Jerusalem had devised a neat trick. If people contributed to the Temple what they would have used to support their parents, then that gift, according to these priests, became "corban"—an acceptable offering to God. It excused them from fulfilling the

Law, and, incidentally, fattened the treasury of the
Temple.

So it was that Jesus said of the Pharisees, "In vain do they
worship me" (verse 9). They taught the traditions of men
as though they were the Law of God.

There is another kind of worship, besides mere lip
service, that Jesus called vain in His sight, and that is the
substitution of our traditions, however venerable, for
obedience to the Word and the commandment of Almighty
God.

After Jesus' condemnation of the Pharisees, the disciples
approached Jesus and whispered in His ear, "You know
You're making them very mad?" And Jesus responded,
"Every plant which my heavenly Father has not planted
will be rooted up" (Matthew 16:13).

Do you see that, in all our ecclesiastical traditions, there
are trees that are not of God's planting? Are we to expect
that ritual and ceremony, as a replacement for worship
that rises out of the depths of our beings, represents an
acceptable substitute in the sight of the holy God? I think
not.

The third passage is from John's Gospel. The woman at
the well asked Jesus where the appropriate location was—
whether in Jerusalem or on Mount Gerizim—to worship
God. She was surprised by His answer.

> "The hour is coming, and now is, when the true
> worshipers will worship the Father in spirit and
> truth, for such the Father seeks to worship him"
> (John 4:23).

There is a kind of worship, you see, that God hates—one
pronounced vain and empty before Him—and another
kind of worship God longs for. Here, Jesus describes that
latter as worship in spirit and in truth.

What does it mean to worship God in truth?

The Greek word here for "truth" is *alethia*, based on *lethos*, meaning veil. The *a* is a negative element (just as *theos* is the word for God, and an atheist is a person who does not believe in God), so that *alethia* means "without a veil."

Elsewhere Jesus said, "I am the truth" (John 14:6), and "He who has seen me has seen the Father" (John 14:9). Jesus was Truth incarnate, and the Scripture bears testimony to Him as the Truth of God.

So I believe that worship that is pleasing and acceptable in the sight of God is worship that centers in Jesus Christ and is in harmony with holy Scripture.

But Jesus also said we must worship God in spirit. What does that mean? Happily, St. Paul helps us out:

> "I appeal to you therefore, brethren, by the mercies of God, to present your bodies as a living sacrifice, holy and acceptable to God, which is your spiritual worship" (Romans 12:1).

What is spiritual worship? It is the offering of our lives unto the Lord.

No husband can do that for his wife. No wife can do that for her husband. No parents can do that for their children. No clergyman can do that for his congregation. Whether or not we offer ourselves unto the Lord is an intensely personal decision that each one of us must make for ourselves.

You see, God asks of us the oblation of our lives presented to Him—our defeats as well as our victories, our sorrows as well as our joys. Without the presentation of your entire life to the Lord God, true worship has not taken place.

What about praise? Praise is the spontaneous overflow of enjoyment. We praise God when we begin to enjoy Him.

And when we begin to enjoy Him, we will inevitably praise Him.

What about worship? Worship that is a matter of words alone is unacceptable in the sight of our God. Worship that substitutes our traditions for obedience to God's Word is also unacceptable before our God. He seeks worship that is in truth and in spirit.

O God, give us that grace to be able to worship You in a way that delights Your heart; in a way that's in harmony with Your Word; and in a way that arises from the very depths of our being. Through Christ we pray, Amen.

III

Jesus Is Lord

"Let this mind be in you, which was also in Christ Jesus:
Who, being in the form of God, thought it not robbery to
be equal with God:
But made himself of no reputation, and took upon him the
form of a servant, and was made in the likeness of men:
And being found in fashion as a man, he humbled
himself, and became obedient unto death, even the death of
the cross.
Wherefore God also hath highly exalted him, and given
him a name which is above every name:
That at the name of Jesus every knee should bow, of
things in heaven, and things in earth, and things under the
earth;
And that every tongue should confess that Jesus Christ is
Lord" *(Philippians 2: 5-11).*

If you read in the newspaper tomorrow that it had been
proven conclusively no one by the name of Gautama

Buddha ever lived, it wouldn't change a single thing for a Buddhist. The Buddhist religion, you see, is based on the teachings of the Enlightened One, and if Buddha didn't say them, someone else did.

Or if tomorrow you were to read in the newspaper that no one by the name of Confucius ever lived, it would change nothing for a practitioner of that faith, because the ethical system is based on the so-called analects of Confucius. And again, if he didn't originate them, someone else did.

But if tomorrow it were discovered that Jesus Christ never lived, Christianity would collapse in an instant. Why? Because the essence of the Christian faith is not found in the teachings of Jesus, as important as those are, but rather in the Person of Jesus. He is God's Word to us.

Two passages of Scripture depict Jesus as God's special message to the human race. First, listen to the opening words of the letter to the Hebrews:

> "In many and various ways, God spoke of old to
> our fathers by the prophets; but in these last
> days he has spoken unto us by a Son" (Hebrews
> 1:1-2).

These words tell us something we need to remember—that ours is a God who has spoken. In times past, He spoke secondhand, as it were, through the prophets. In these last days, He has spoken to us by His Son.

The theologians have a word for this—they call it revelation. This means that the God we're talking about is not the product of our own imagination, nor the product of mere intellectual hypothesis. Rather, He is a God who has addressed us out of the silence of eternity.

In John 1:1 we read: "In the beginning was the Word, and the Word was with God, and the Word was God."

I am sure that, as John began his Gospel, he had in the back of his mind the way the Bible starts: "In the beginning, God." (You will turn to Scripture in vain to discover any formal argument for God's existence. That is simply assumed on every page, and presented to us in the very first verse as the great presupposition of everything else.)

Now what is a word? A word is a means of communication. Whether it is spoken or written (as these words are), the purpose of a word is to transmit understanding.

"In the beginning was the Word," wrote John, "and the Word was with God"—indicating some kind of plurality—"and the Word was God"—indicating unity.

And then it all comes together:

> "And the Word became flesh and dwelt among us " (verse 14).

Here we stand on holy ground! This Word, which *was* God and was *with* Him throughout all eternity, became flesh and lived among us. Theologians have a term for this, too—they call it the Incarnation. And it is because of this that Christianity differs from all other religions of the world.

God's message to the human race, you see, is not a doctrine, an idea, a teaching, a principle, or a philosophy. It is a Person, a Word become flesh, and we know Him as Jesus Christ.

There are two questions I want us to consider in this chapter: who is this Jesus; and what is His place in God's plan?

Listen to St. Paul:

> "For he has made known to us in all wisdom and insight the mystery of his will..." (Ephesians 1:9a).

Did you hear that? God has revealed to us already the

mystery of His will! That means that you and I do not need to gaze into a crystal ball to try to figure out what God is up to. Nor do we have to hazard any guesses as to what He may be about. He has revealed His will to us already,

> "...according to his purpose which he set forth in Christ" (verse 9b).

The will of God, in other words, centers in Jesus Christ. If we leave Jesus out of our consideration of what God is doing, we'll never understand it.

Now, what is this will? It is

> "...a plan for the fullness of time, to unite all things in him, things in heaven and things on earth" (verse 10).

God's announced plan is to unite all things in Christ one day. Everything. Everything in heaven, and everything on earth.

And he tells us how this can come about:

> "According to the working of [God's] great might which he accomplished in Christ when he raised him from the dead and made him sit at his right hand in heavenly places, far above all rule and authority and power and dominion, and above every name that is named, not only in this age, but also in that which is to come " (verses 19-21).

Think, for a minute, of the various power structures in our world. Think of the whole realm of business and finance; of governments and legislatures and laws and officials. Think of entertainment and the arts. This passage is telling us that God has raised His Son to a place of authority above all authorities, of power above all powers, and of dominion above all dominions. There will never arise another person whose excellence exceeds that of the Lord Jesus Christ.

So the Father

> "has put all things under his feet and made him
> the head over all things for the church, which is
> his body" (verse 22).

This is not, I admit, the way it looks right now. Most of the world is unaware of the fact that God has made Jesus Head over all things; that God's plan centers in Jesus Christ's bringing everything in heaven and on earth into unity under His authority.

But the fact that it doesn't look that way now doesn't matter. This is a plan, you see, for the fullness of time. It will require all of human history, from creation to consummation, for this plan to be completed.

But let's look at the first question I raised a few pages back: Who is this Jesus, anyway—this Person in whom God's plan centers?

> "He is the image of the invisible God"
> (Colossians 1:15).

Have you wondered what God looks like? Look into the face of Jesus Christ. He is, in the words of Hebrews 1:3, "the express image" of the Father. That's why Jesus could say, "He who has seen me has seen the Father" (John 14:9).

Our Colossians passage proclaims this, saying,

> "For in Him all things were created, in heaven

and on earth, visible and invisible, whether
thrones or dominions or principalities or authorities—all things were created through Him and
for Him" (verse 16).

I know that, traditionally, we attribute creation to God
the Father. But the New Testament takes great pains to
tell us that God created the universe by His Word. (God
said, "Let there be light," and there was light. God said,
"Let dry land appear," and it appeared.) As John wrote, "All
things were made through him"—that is to say, through
the Word—"and without him was not anything made that
was made" (John 1:3).

That same Word, then, that spoke the universe into
existence is the Word that became incarnate in Jesus
Christ.

So Paul concludes the Colossians passage:

"He is the head of the body, the church; he is the
beginning, the firstborn from the dead, that in
everything he might be preeminent" (verse 18).

May I tell you what has become the deepest conviction of
my heart? I believe it is the will of our God that His Son,
Jesus, be exalted as Head over everything—that in everything He might be preeminent.

Why? Because the Father has decreed that the day will
come when everything in heaven and earth finds its unity,
its significance and its meaning in Jesus; because the Father
has placed all things under Jesus' feet, and has elevated
Him to a place at His right hand, far above all human rule
or power or dominion or authority; because Jesus is the
Head of all things.

But now let's consider another passage, so we might
understand more fully who this Jesus is, and where He fits

into God's plan. It's found in Philippians in St. Paul's account of the Christmas story, without any mention of angels, or shepherds, or Bethlehem, or any of the familiar accoutrements of that story.

> "Have this mind among yourselves which you have in Christ Jesus, who, though he was in the form of God, did not count equality with God a thing to be grasped, but emptied himself, taking the form of a servant, being born in the likeness of men" (Philippans 2:5-7).

In coming into the world, you see, Jesus did not give up his deity, merely all the prerogatives of deity. He "emptied" Himself, becoming a human being among us—and not only that, but a servant.

Since the special attitude of a servant is one of obedience, we read:

> "And being found in human form he humbled himself and became obedient unto death, even death on a cross. Therefore God has highly exalted him and bestowed on him the name which is above every name, that at the name of Jesus every knee should bow, in heaven and on earth and under the earth, and every tongue confess that Jesus Christ is Lord, to the glory of God the Father" (verses 8-11).

Where is human history moving? What is the denouement of God's great cosmic drama?

It is that day, already decreed by the Father, when He will raise from the dead all who have ever lived; and in that day all will bow before Jesus Christ.

Not all will bow willingly. For some it will be a revelation of judgment. For others it will be a time of great joy. But all will bow, and every tongue confess that Jesus Christ is Lord, to the glory of God the Father.

Perhaps you're saying to yourself, "If we elevate Jesus that high, doesn't it do violence to the glory of the Father?"

Let me say quickly that there is no jealousy in the God-head. Notice again how the passage ends: *To the glory of God the Father*. How do we glorify God the Father? By exalting God the Son. God has set the universe up that way.

Some others of you might wonder, "If that's true, doesn't exalting Jesus so high do violence to the glory of the Holy Spirit?" But remember what Jesus said of the coming of the Spirit: "When the Spirit of truth comes ... he will glorify me" (John 16:13-14).

So you see, whether you look from the point of view of the Father or from that of the Holy Spirit, it all adds up to the same thing. It is God's desire that His Son, Jesus, be declared as Lord of heaven and earth.

To conclude this chapter, let's look together at a dream recorded 2,500 years ago by the Old Testament prophet, Daniel—a dream that has yet to be fulfilled.

> "I saw in the night visions, and behold, with the clouds of heaven there came one like a son of man, and he came to the Ancient of Days and was presented before him. And to him was given dominion and glory and kingdom, that all peoples, nations, and languages should serve him; his dominion is an everlasting dominion, which shall not pass away, and his kingdom one that shall not be destroyed" (Daniel 7:13-14).

Do you get the picture? We are peering into a vast heavenly throne room where the Lord God, the Ancient of Days, is seated. And, 'way at the other end of the room, the doors open, and one is ushered in like the Son of Man.

Daniel, by the power of the Holy Spirit, was able to

describe for us the last act in our great cosmic drama, when all might and majesty and power and dominion will be given to the Son.

A final vision is recorded for us in the New Testament, with an awesome depiction of what lies ahead:

> "Then I looked, and I heard around the throne and the living creatures and the elders the voice of many angels, numbering myriads of myriads and thousands and thousands, saying with a loud voice, 'Worthy is the Lamb who was slain, to receive power and wealth and wisdom and might and honor and glory and blessing!' And I heard every creature in heaven and on earth and under the earth and in the sea, and all therein, saying, 'To him who sits upon the throne and to the Lamb be blessing and honor and glory and might for ever and ever!' And the four living creatures said, 'Amen!' and the elders fell down and worshiped" (Revelation 5:11-14).

Understand, dear friends, that it is the plan of God that His Son be elevated to the place of absolute supremacy in the universe. Understand that you and I have the opportunity now to live under His Lordship. And remember that the universal anthem one day on every tongue will be, *Jesus Christ is Lord!*

IV

The Peace That Passes Understanding

"Rejoice in the Lord alway: and again I say rejoice.
Let your moderation be known unto all men. The Lord is
at hand.
Be careful for nothing; but in every thing by prayer and
supplication with thanksgiving let your requests' be made
known unto God.
And the peace of God, which passeth all understanding,
shall keep your hearts and minds through Christ Jesus"
                                    (Philippians 4:4-7).

Was there ever a time in the long history of the human race when the desire for peace was more fervent? Everyone talks of peace. Everyone longs for it. And yet, despite all our efforts, it seems to slip through our fingers and remain as elusive as ever. What is this peace that is so fervently sought and so rarely found?

Let me offer a simple definition of peace, which applies whether one is speaking of accord among nations, harmony within families, even healing of the generation

41

gap. Peace is the cessation of hostilities; the breaking down
of walls of separation; the healing of breaches; the achieve-
ment of unity out of chaos, and harmony out of discord;
the substitution of mutual trust for suspicion; the making
of enemies into friends.

The Bible has reduced all the misery of mankind to a
single cause: sin. Sin has left in its wake an endless
succession of broken relationships and fractured fellow-
ships. It has driven wedges between husbands and wives,
parents and children, teachers and students. It has divided
people into warring groups, each demanding its own rights
and willing to seize them at the expense of others.

Sin has left its damning mark on every area of human
experience, and on three relationships in particular.

First, sin has broken man's relationship with God, so
that the prophet Isaiah declared,

> "Your iniquities have made a separation between
> you and your God, and your sins have hid his face
> from you so that he does not hear" (Isaiah 59:2).

Second, sin has disrupted the inner harmony within
each of our individual lives, so that man is at war with
himself. St. Paul recognized the destructive power of sin in
his own life, and cried out in despair:

> "I do not understand my own actions. For I do not
> what I want, but I do the very thing I hate ... I can
> will what is right, but I cannot do it. For I do not
> do the good I want, but the evil I do not want is
> what I do" (Romans 7:15, 18, 19).

Third, sin has splintered relationships among men and
nations. In his epistle, James recognized the impossibility
of creating a peaceful society because of the disharmony
embedded in the very heart of man.

> "What causes wars, and what causes fightings
> among you? Is it not your passions that are at
> war in your members? You desire and do not
> have; so you kill. And you covet and cannot
> obtain; so you fight and wage war" (James 4:1-2).

The Bible pictures man apart from God's grace as engaged in an intense and bitter warfare, fighting an endless battle on three fronts at the same time: man at war with God; man at war with himself; and man at war with his neighbor. Peace, if there is ever to be any peace, must be established on all three levels.

May I say right here that the Bible is not only devastatingly frank in its analysis of human misery and the ravaging effects of sin, it is also gloriously clear in setting forth the only cure for man's warring madness—and His name is Jesus Christ.

Christ is the answer to man's quest for peace—whether it be with God, peace with himself or peace with his neighbor—because it is through Christ that God has dealt forever with the problem of sin.

"He himself," according to St. Peter, "bore our sins in his body on the tree, that we might die to sin and live to righteousness" (1 Peter 2:24). Again, he says, "For Christ also died for sins once for all, the righteous for the unrighteous, that he might bring us to God" (1 Peter 3:18). And St. Paul says further, "He gave himself for our sins to deliver us from the present evil age, according to the will of our God and Father" (Galatians 1:4).

Jesus Christ, then, is God's answer to man's sin, and it is through Him that we can find the peace for which we so desperately long. St. Paul says this:

> "But now in Christ Jesus, you who once were far
> off have been brought near in the blood of
> Christ. For he is our peace, who has made us both

one, and has broken down the dividing wall of
hostility...so making peace" (Ephesians 2:13-
15).

The peace that Jesus Christ brings pervades all three
areas of man's estrangement, and restores our fellowship
with God, ourselves and our neighbors. Let's look at each
one of these in turn.

The great principle of the Bible, first of all, from the
opening pages of Genesis to the closing pages of Revelation, is that man's sin has built a wall of separation between
him and God. The thundering words of the Lord to Ezekiel
crash down upon our ears in dreadful judgment:

> "The soul that sinneth, it shall die" (Ezekiel
> 18:20).

What's more, man from his side of the great wall of
separation can do nothing to cross over. There is no
sacrifice God will accept, no prayer God will hear save,
"Lord, be merciful to me, a sinner."

But listen to the words of Paul in II Corinthian 5:18-19:

> "All this is from God, who through Christ
> reconciled us to himself and gave us the ministry
> of reconciliation; that is, God was in Christ
> reconciling the world to himself, not counting
> their trespasses against them."

To reconcile means to remove enmity between parties at
variance with each other—in this case, God and man. In
the Bible, moreover, it is what God does, never what man
does, that brings about reconciliation. The enmity
between God and man is removed by an act of God. Reconciliation was made possible through the death of Jesus
Christ.

> "Therefore, since we are justified by faith, we
> have peace with God through our Lord Jesus
> Christ" (Romans 5:1).

There you have it! By believing in Christ, we can find
peace with God, the forgiveness of sins, and the gift of
eternal life.

Second, let's consider peace with ourselves. The Bible
teaches that man apart from God's grace is fighting a
constant battle within himself. Right in the depths of
individual human consciousness, we feel an inner division
that is sometimes so acute that it could be described as
warfare.

Freudian psychoanalysis says it is the struggle between
the id and the superego. Christian theology calls it the con-
flict between the innate moral nature within man because
he is created in the image of God, and the sinful propen-
sities that are his because of original sin.

We have all sensed that feeling of being torn in two. It is
what people mean when they say there is a little of the
devil and a little of the angel in all of us.

Only Jesus Christ can unify the personality and set it
moving in one direction. He alone is the answer to man's
sense of inner disharmony and division.

In light of this truth, however, let's look at a puzzling
statement of Jesus that seems to violate everything we've
just said. He told His disciples:

> "You must not think that I have come to bring
> peace to the earth. I have not come to bring
> peace, but a sword" (Matthew 10:34).

On the surface, this passage appears to contradict all we
know about Jesus Christ. Is He not called the Prince of
Peace? Did not the angels sing at His birth, "Peace on earth

among men of good will?" Did He not reassure His
disciples, "Peace I leave with you; my peace I give to you"?

The meaning of this perplexing statement becomes clear
as we look at what follows it. Jesus continued:

> "I have come to set a man against his father, a
> daughter against her mother, a son's wife
> against her mother-in-law; and a man will find
> his enemies under his own roof. No man is
> worthy of me who cares more for son or
> daughter; no man is worthy of me who does not
> take up his cross and walk in my footsteps. By
> gaining his life a man will lose it; by losing his life
> for my sake, he will gain it" (verses 35-39).

Jesus is really speaking of priorities. Here He claims His
own rightful place as the sovereign Lord of our lives, and
He will settle for nothing less.

Jesus is doing two things: making a claim about Himself,
and issuing a demand. His claim is that, as man's Redeemer
and the incarnate Son of God, He has the right to assume
the position of Lord in our lives. (We admit this each time
we call Him the *Lord* Jesus Christ.) His demand is that all
else in our life take second place. Only in this way can our
inner lives be united and move forward in a single
direction.

There is something strange and wonderful about the
Lordship of Christ. As we seek to give Him first place in
our lives, other considerations begin to fall into place. So it
was that Jesus promised, "Seek ye first the kingdom of
God, and his righteousness; and all these things shall be
added unto you" (Matthew 6:33).

It is all a matter of priorities. Put first things first. Give
Jesus first place. Make Him the magnificent obsession of
your life, and He will give you peace in your inward being.
He will establish order and harmony in your life. And as

you put Jesus Christ squarely on the throne and seek to live for Him, the peace of God which passes all understanding will begin to flood your inner self and bring rest to your soul.

Finally, let's consider peace with our neighbors, whether our neighbor be the man next door, the couple down the street, or the people on the other side of the world.

It is my job to point out that, apart from Jesus Christ and the peace He can bring, the possibility of attaining lasting peace among men is very slight. Jesus Himself said that we should expect wars and rumors of wars until the very end of the age.

The reason is that man is able to treat only the symptoms and not the disease. The disease in this case is sin—the sin that builds walls of separation between man and God, man and himself, and man and his neighbor.

There is a definite order to be followed, then, in the quest for peace. First, a person must find peace with God, which cannot be made apart from Jesus Christ, mankind's Savior and God's remedy for sin. Second, the disharmony at the heart of every individual must be healed, which can occur only through the Lordship of Christ in our lives. Then and only then is it possible to achieve a lasting peace among men.

It is the same with love. Our first priority is to love God with all our heart, soul and mind. Until God is given first place in life, man's estimate of himself is bound to be wrong. He will either overestimate his own importance and set himself up as God (in the language of philosophy this is called Titanism), or he will underestimate his place in the universe and see himself as one among the animals.

A Christian is freed from both incorrect evaluations. Because he has given Jesus first place, he can look at himself as a being created in the image of God with a dignity that sets him apart from the rest of the created order. Because he has been redeemed by Jesus Christ, he can see himself as infinitely valuable in the sight of God.

Because God has accepted me through Jesus Christ, I am now free to accept myself; I can face squarely my assets and liabilities as a person. And, with the continuing help of the Holy Spirit, I can begin to grow in grace, and in knowledge and favor with God and man.

In stating that we are to love our neighbor as ourselves, Jesus recognized a profound truth: that we are not free to love our neighbor until we have a proper estimate of ourselves. Similarly, in terms of peace, we will never cultivate peace among men until we have found peace in our own hearts.

It is right here that the great promise of Jesus comes to the fore:

"Peace I leave with you; my peace I give to you" (John 14:27).

Jesus came to break down the wall of separation between God and man by making peace through His own death on the cross. Jesus came to bring peace to the troubled and divided soul by assuming Lordship over our lives and bringing unity out of chaos. Finally, Jesus came to bring peace among men of good will—men who have been reconciled to God and also with themselves.

Tell me, how do things stand with you and the peace of God? Have you been reconciled to God through faith in His Son, Jesus Christ? Does the peace of God, which passes all understanding, keep your heart and mind in the knowledge and love of God and His Son, Jesus Christ our Lord?

And how do you stand with your neighbor? Is the peace of God being shed abroad in your heart and life, renewing and healing the relationships you have with people every day?

If the answer to these questions is "yes," then praise God for His graciousness in your life!

If the answer is no, then I commend to you once again Jesus Christ, the Prince of Peace, who has reconciled us to the Father through His death on the cross; who seeks to be crowned the Lord of our lives, thus quieting the tempest in our hearts; and who seeks to create among men a fellowship of the redeemed who shall live to His glory, forever and ever.

V

If Christ Be Not Raised

"Now if Christ be preached that he rose from the dead, how say some among you that there is no resurrection of the dead?

But if there be no resurrection of the dead, then is Christ not risen:

And if Christ be not risen, then is our preaching vain, and your faith is also vain.

Yea, and we are found false witnesses of God; because we have testified of God that he raised up Christ: whom he raised not up, if so be that the dead rise not.

For if the dead rise not, then is not Christ raised:

And if Christ be not raised, your faith is vain; ye are yet in your sins.

Then they also which are fallen asleep in Christ are perished.

If in this life only we have hope in Christ, we are of all men most miserable.

But now is Christ risen from the dead, and become the firstfruits of them that slept" (I Corinthians 15:12-20).

One of the most pathetic sentences ever uttered came surprisingly enough from a cynical, cold-blooded Roman. This man had been commissioned to maintain the dignity of an empire and the might of Caesar among a conquered people. He was powerful and proud—not the type you could readily imagine uttering anything pathetic. His name was Pontius Pilate.

On the day at hand, his subordinates were badgering him about the necessity of doing something immediately, now that Jesus was dead and put away in the tomb. There had been rumors that He had said He would rise from the dead on the third day. So Pilate's advisers wanted to ensure that there be no tricks at the grave, no rifling of the sepulchre, no concocting of tales by His friends to the effect that He was not dead.

"You must do something to prevent that, Pilate," they urged him. "You must take precautions at the tomb."

Then it came, this most pathetic sentence of all time.

"You have a guard of soldiers," Pilate responded. "Go, make it as secure as you can" (Matthew 27:65).

Now, if you were to watch a man advance into the gray of the dawn and shout to the sun, "Stop! Today you shall not climb the heavens nor traverse the sky," what would you think of that man?

Or if you were standing on the shore when the tide had ebbed and begun to return, and you saw a man draw a line in the sand, and then cry to the waves that were heaving their shoulders for a new advance, "Halt! You shall not pass this line," what would you say of such a man? Surely you would think him mad.

What will you say then to this pathetic Roman who thought he could barricade the tomb of the Son of God?

But wait a minute. Perhaps Pilate was not mad after all. For what is it that we are asked to believe? Is it that someone who was once dead—and not only dead but also buried and placed in a tomb—actually came forth from the grave alive, and is not only alive, but alive forevermore? Is not this what we are asked to believe?

Perhaps it is we who are mad. Perhaps we are the pathetic ones, we who gather year by year to celebrate the festival of the resurrection.

Perhaps Pilate's advisers were right: "Let there be no tampering with the tomb, no rifling of the sepulchre, no concocting of stories about a resurrection. Do something, Pilate. For if Christ is not alive from the dead, then you are doing the human race a service. Destroy the idea before it ever begins to take root in the human mind; before people ever begin to build their hopes on it. Make them face it, Pilate. Because if Christ is not raised from the dead, then death is the absolute end, and the quicker we realize it, the better."

The odd thing about it is, the New Testament actually agrees with these words of Pilate's advisers. St. Paul himself discussed the issue.

> "If Christ be not risen, then is our preaching vain, and your faith is also vain. Yea, and we are found false witnesses of God; because we have testified of God that he raised up Christ: whom he raised not up, if so be that the dead rise not. For if the dead rise not, then is not Christ raised: And if Christ be not raised, your faith is vain; ye are yet in your sins. Then they also which are fallen asleep in Christ are perished. If in this life only we have hope in Christ, we are of all men most miserable" (I Corinthians 15:14-19).

Well may we shudder to consider these consequences! John Henry Newman, a theologian of the last century, once imagined what it would be like to look out into the world and see no trace of God at all. That would be, he wrote, just as if he were to look into a mirror and not see his own face.

Think of it—looking straight into a mirror and seeing only a blank. It is that same shudder of soul that the apostle Paul's words here create: "If Christ be not raised."

Or think of this: suppose that one day this earth were suddenly to break out of its orbit and, released from the gravitational pull of the sun, fly off at a tangent, farther and farther into the cold immensities of space. Men would wait, wonderingly, for the coming of the spring, for the birds' return, and the buds on the trees. But there would be no sign of spring; only deeper and ever deeper winter.

"Surely tomorrow," they would say, "we'll awake to a breath of springtime." But spring would never come; only a deathly cold gripping the earth, until at last the truth would break in upon them: "We are doomed."

It is the same cold shudder of the soul that meets us here: "If Christ be not raised."

Yet here it is on the pages of the holy Scripture. It seems evident that the Holy Spirit would have us consider the implications of a world that had never heard the voice of the angel announcing, "He is not here; for he has risen, as he said" (Matthew 28:6).

There would be three main consequences of such an eventuality. First, "If Christ be not raised . . . your faith is vain," Paul wrote. All the trust you had ever put in God would be one huge mistake; all the brave confidence you had cherished would be smashed, torn to shreds, blown into thin air. Your faith would be gone, finished.

Do you not see why? Then look at Jesus. Here was a man who lived an absolutely perfect life. Here was a man who trusted all His life that God would deliver Him; that God would not suffer His Holy One to see corruption. Jesus was crucified, died, and was buried.

And if God did nothing? You could never trust God after that, Paul is saying, neither His love nor His power.

Some 1500 years ago, someone read the story of the death of Jesus Christ to Clovis, the king of the Franks. Clovis was no Christian; he was at that time still a barbarian.

Yet, as the story went on, Clovis reached for his sword, drew it out and cried, "Oh, if only I had been there with my Franks! We would have charged up the slopes of Calvary, smashed those Romans, and saved His life."

If God Himself did nothing at all, but let His only Son remain in the grave—His Son who had died with faith in His heart and forgiveness on His lips—then what kind of God would that be? You may as well make up your mind to it: your faith would be in vain.

Nor could you trust in God's power, for the clash at Calvary involved not only Jesus and His enemies, but God and all the forces of evil. If the cross had been the end of the story, the sealed tomb the final chapter in this unhappy drama, then perhaps you can imagine the celebration in the halls of Hell that night. "We win!" they would have cried. "God is blotted out."

Indeed, Paul is saying, "If Christ be not raised," then don't even speak of God's power. Your faith is vain.

Perhaps you are inclined to ask, "So what does it matter? Is our faith in God such an important thing that we would suffer terribly if we were to lose it?"

One famous German drew an imaginative picture of Jesus returning to the earth and confessing that all His teaching about God had been mistaken; that He had discovered there was no Father behind things after all, and that He thought it best to come back and tell men so.

All the world hearing that broke down and wept.

It does matter. Life without faith is not worth the living. And yet if Christ be not raised, the foundation for faith is gone.

If, on the other hand, Christ is risen from the dead, then faith in God is crowned, justified, vindicated. Then, in the blackest of days, you can shout with the apostle Paul:

> "For I am persuaded, that neither death, nor life,
> nor angels, nor principalities, nor powers, nor
> things present, nor things to come, nor height,
> nor depth, nor any other creature, shall be able to
> separate us from the love of God, which is in
> Christ Jesus our Lord" (Romans 8:38-39).

Let's consider the second main consequence Paul draws:
"If Christ be not raised ... ye are yet in your sins."

All this talk of forgiveness, in that case, would be pure
delusion! Any words about God's putting our sins behind
His back; or drowning them in the depths of the sea; or
removing them as far from us as the east is from the west;
or making the crimsoned pages of our lives as white as
snow—all these words would be mockery. We would yet be
guilty, and there would be no escape—none at all.

Do you see why? Because if the cross were the end of the
story, then Christ's brave but pathetic attempt to be a
Savior failed. Because the sins of men that slew Him had
the last word. Jesus, seeing sin and its deadly heritage
through the generations, threw His own body across its
path, trying to stem the rising tide. But He was broken by
it, and we are still in our sins.

Once we see what is really at stake here, we will understand that forgiveness is something we cannot live
without. You and I simply cannot make it without the
possibility of starting over again. Yet "if Christ be not
raised," that possibility is gone, and we are dead in our sins.

But if Christ is risen from the dead, then sin is defeated!
It has met its match. It has been broken, blotted out, and
we are free.

How beautifully this was expressed by John Bunyan in
The Pilgrim's Progress:

"He ran thus till he came at a place somewhat ascending, and upon that place stood a cross, and a little below in the bottom, a sepulchre. So I saw in my dream that just as Christian came up with the cross, his burden loosed from off his shoulders, and fell from off his back, and began to tumble, and so continued to do, till it came to the mouth of the sepulchre where it fell in, and I saw it no more.

"Then was Christian glad and lightsome, and said with a merry heart, 'He hath given me rest, by his sorrow, and life, by his death.' Then he stood still awhile to look and wonder...."

All that, if Christ be *raised* from the dead!
Let's consider the final consequence Paul draws:

"If Christ be not raised...then they also which are fallen asleep in Christ are perished."

How else can I put it? Perished! Dead! Finished! When a man dies, he is dead like a dog.

Surely the venerable Bede was right when he pictured human life without the resurrection as a bird that flies out of inky darkness into a window of a brilliantly lighted banqueting hall, darts across that brilliance for a moment, then out another window into the blackness of night, forever.

Only a cruel God could put such love and longing into our hearts, then extinguish it abruptly. Surely this is how we would feel if death finished love and destroyed it forever.

And let us be perfectly clear: "If Christ be not raised," then death is the end. Our loved ones, and we ourselves, will utterly perish—cast, as Tennyson put it, as rubbish to the void.

Do you not see why? For if Jesus never rose from the dead, how ever should we? If the only perfect life that ever lived was crushed by death, how can we escape? Death would be the end. All would indeed perish.

"Does it really matter?" you ask.

Do not make a mockery of life. So long as there is love, so long as parents beget children, so long as one human heart cleaves to another, we might rather ask if anything *else* really matters. If all our loves, hopes, dreams and aspirations end in the grave, then St. Paul is right: "We are of all men most miserable."

But if Christ be raised from the dead, then all is changed. Oh yes, there are still sadness and tears when we stand in the presence of death. But the sting is gone. And death, for the one whose life is hid with Christ in God, represents entrance into the nearer presence of God.

Do you remember how D. L. Moody, the great American evangelist, died? These were his last words: "Don't weep for me. Earth is receding, heaven is advancing. Rejoice! This is my coronation day."

Oliver Cromwell, as he lay dying, looked into the sad faces of the people surrounding his bed and said to them, "Is there no one here who will praise the Lord?"

Praise in the face of death—yes, that's it! That is the glory of the resurrection.

So in this passage Paul has confronted head on the grim thought, "what if Christ had not risen?" and drawn from it three inevitable conclusions: That faith would be gone; forgiveness would be gone; and eternal life would be gone.

Then, while the shudder of such a loss is still passing through his readers, there comes the sudden burst of triumph. Each word rings out like a trumpet blast, a shout, a battle cry:

"But now is Christ risen from the dead"
(I Corinthians 15:20).

If you were to ask Paul, "How do you know?" he would reply, "Know? Why, I've spoken with men who have seen Him—Peter, Andrew, James, John, and a hundred others—men whose whole lives were changed by the risen Christ."

Even more than this, Paul's testimony was not second-hand. "Not alive?" he would exclaim. "Why, Jesus stopped me on my way to Damascus one day, and my life has never been the same. Now I preach the very message I once sought to destroy."

The goal of Paul's life, as he wrote in Philippians 3:10, was "that I may know Christ, and the power of his resurrection, and the fellowship of his sufferings, being made conformable unto his death."

He also wrote:

"It is no longer I who live, but Christ who lives in me; and the life I now live in the flesh I live by faith in the Son of God, who loved me and gave himself for me" (Galatians 2:20).

You were wrong, Pilate. Your orders were in vain. "You have a guard of soldiers," you told them. "Make the tomb as secure as you can."

Such pathos! For God Himself rolled the stone away, the guards fell back as dead men, and the Son of God stepped forth to live forevermore.

"Thanks be to God, who gives us the victory through our Lord Jesus Christ!" (I Corinthians 15:57).

VI

Freed To Serve

"This then is the message which we have heard of him, and declare unto you, that God is light, and in him is no darkness at all.

If we say that we have fellowship with him, and walk in darkness, we lie, and do not the truth:

But if we walk in the light, as he is in the light, we have fellowship one with another, and the blood of Jesus Christ his Son cleanseth us from all sin.

If we say that we have no sin, we deceive ourselves, and the truth is not in us.

If we confess our sins, he is faithful and just to forgive us our sins, and to cleanse us from all unrighteousness.

If we say that we have not sinned, we make him a liar, and his word is not in us" (I John 1:5-10).

Carl Sandburg, in his monumental biography of Abraham Lincoln, tells of an incident in the life of that great President that occurred during the Civil War and before the abolition of slavery.

Lincoln had gone to a slave auction in nearby Virginia, and there purchased a young slave girl for the sole purpose of setting her free. The girl did not know who had bought her, nor did she know why. She simply assumed it was another business transaction in which she, as someone's personal property, was changing hands.

After Lincoln paid the auctioneer, he was given ownership papers on which he wrote a few words and signed his name. Then he walked up to the girl, handed her the papers and said, "These are your papers of freedom. Now you are free to go."

The girl did not understand what was happening.

"Free?" she asked. "What do you mean?"

So the President began to explain to her gently and with great compassion, "You have been a slave all your life, but today I paid the price for your life, and you are free to go wherever you want. Never again will you have to be a slave to any man."

For a moment the girl was silent, as it began to dawn on her what wonderful thing had happened.

Finally she looked full into the face of that great President and said, "If it is true that I am now free, and can go wherever I want, and do whatever I wish, then I want to stay with you forever, and serve you until I die."

Legally she was free, but love and gratitude had bound her in a new and willing service.

It should not be difficult for Christians to understand the experience of this young slave girl for we, like her, have exchanged the bonds of slavery for the cords of love. We have been liberated from the bondage of sin and death, and committed voluntarily to Jesus Christ, our new Master.

As we look at the experience of this young girl, we can see that she passed through three stages. First, she experienced bondage, about which she herself could do nothing, and from which she was unable to extricate herself. Second, she underwent deliverance, brought about by the intervention of President Lincoln, who in compassion paid the price to set her free. Finally, she chose to serve him voluntarily in love.

In this chapter, I would like to focus our attention on these three stages—bondage, deliverance and voluntary service in love—as illustrative of our relationship to Almighty God.

The Bible describes man's natural condition apart from Christ as one of bondage—bondage to sin and death. Our experience parallels that of this girl in at least two respects.

First of all, she was probably born into the condition of slavery. It was not as though she had been free once and then, through some misfortune, lost her freedom and became a slave. No, she was a slave because she was born into a race of people that generations before had been reduced to slavery.

The same is true in the life of a Christian. You and I are sinners, not only by choice, but also because we have been born into a race infected by sin from the very beginning.

The Bible defines sin as the transgression of the Law of God. To put it another way, sin is breaking God's commandments. And the greatest commandment, according to Jesus, is this:

> "You shall love the Lord your God with all your heart, and with all your soul, and with all your mind. This is the great and first commandment. And a second is like it, You shall love your neighbor as yourself" (Matthew 22:37-39).

Usually, when you and I think of sin, we think of the grosser sins—murder, or adultery, or robbing a bank. So there are many among us who can say, "I've never done any of those things. I don't feel I'm so much of a sinner."

There are others who feel uncomfortable in having to confess themselves to be miserable offenders. But this is because we persist in thinking of sin exclusively as extreme dereliction or willful delinquency.

Biblically speaking, sin is simply the transgression of the Law. And if the essence of the Law is love for God with all our hearts, souls and minds, and love for our neighbor as ourselves, then who among us can escape the charge of sin?

I know that seldom, if ever, do I love God with my whole heart, soul and mind; and rarely do I love my neighbor as myself.

So sin is universal. It is not just a set of specific offenses, but a condition that includes every one of us by virtue of belonging to the human race. Paul said that "all have sinned and fall short of the glory of God" (Romans 3:23). The psalmist declared, "They are all alike corrupt; there is none that does good, no, not one" (Psalm 14:3). And the prophet Isaiah wrote, "All we like sheep have gone astray; we have turned every one to his own way" (Isaiah 53:6).

Sin as the condition into which we were born is the first way we parallel the experience of the young slave girl. The second is that we are not only sinners, but enslaved to sin in a state of bondage from which we can do nothing to free ourselves. As Jesus taught, "Everyone who commits sin is a slave to sin" (John 8:34).

This being so, we are also enslaved to death as the consequence of sin. Recall what the Lord God said to Adam in the Garden of Eden: "For in the day that you eat of [the forbidden fruit] you shall die" (Genesis 2:17). Paul wrote, "Sin came into the world through one man [Adam] and death through sin, and so death spread to all men because all men sinned" (Romans 5:12).

Death, then, is the inevitable result of sin—spiritual death as well as physical death.

If you think back to the experience of Adam and Eve, you

will realize they did not die the same day they disobeyed
God. That is, they did not die physically. They did die
spiritually. Whereas before they had walked and talked
freely with the Lord in the garden, now when they heard
the voice of the Lord calling them, they hid themselves out
of fear. Sin—the disobedience to the commandment of
God—had put this fear into their hearts, for they now
knew themselves to be sinners in the sight of the holy God.
He had become Someone to flee.

You and I have been born, according to the Scriptures,
into a race of men who from birth are spiritually dead.
Ultimately, each of us will also die physically. But if there
are two kinds of death talked about in Scripture, there are
also two kinds of life. One is physical life—which we are
experiencing right now—and the other is spiritual life, the
life of God, which is open and available to all of us.

The only way to receive spiritual life, according to Jesus,
is to be born again. He told Nicodemus,

> "Unless one is born anew, he cannot see the
> kingdom of God.... That which is born of the
> flesh is flesh, and that which is born of the Spirit
> is spirit. Do not marvel that I said to you, 'You
> must be born anew'" (John 3:3, 6-7).

So how does a person escape bondage to sin and death?
This leads us to the second stage of our young friend's
experience—the stage of deliverance, in which Abraham
Lincoln came on the scene, paid the price, and set the slave
girl free.

What a marvelous illustration of what our Lord Jesus
Christ has done for us! Sunday after Sunday, certain
church congregations repeat these words from the Nicene
Creed: "For us and for our salvation, He came down from
heaven." That is why He came—to set us free from
bondage to sin and death.

Do you remember the message the angels spoke to Joseph before the birth of Christ?

"You shall call his name Jesus, for he will save his people from this sins" (Matthew 1:21).

And recall John the Baptist's words to his friends the day he saw Jesus coming over the hillside:

"Behold, the Lamb of God, who takes away the sin of the world" (John 1:29).

No one expressed it any better than the author of the Epistle to the Hebrews, who said that Jesus took upon Himself human nature, "that through death he might destroy him who has the power of death, that is, the devil, and deliver all those who through fear of death were subject to lifelong bondage" (Hebrews 2:14-15).

Jesus came to free us from bondage to sin and death, and the price He paid was His own death on the cross. In the words of the old hymn: "Jesus paid it all, All to Him I owe; Sin had left a crimson stain, He washed it white as snow."

There is one more parallel between our relationship to Jesus Christ as Deliverer and that of this girl to Abraham Lincoln. Even though Lincoln had paid the price and granted her freedom, it would have meant nothing at all had she not believed him, or acted upon what he told her.

So it is with us. It is true that Jesus Christ came into the world to bring eternal life to all men. It is true that He died upon the cross to obtain the forgiveness of everybody's sins. But not everyone inherits eternal life, and not all find their sins forgiven. What is the key?

The key is believing and receiving.

"For God so loved the world, that he gave his only begotten Son, that whosoever believeth in

him should not perish, but have everlasting life"
(John 3:16).

Although the price had been paid and her freedom
granted, if the slave girl had not believed what Lincoln said,
it would have meant nothing. Even though salvation is
offered to us (and by this I mean deliverance from the
bondage of sin and death), unless we act upon it, it will
mean absolutely nothing to us.

Sometimes people ask, "What do you mean by faith?"
The simplest definition I know is this: Faith is taking God
at His word. It is believing what He said.

In the Word we read: "If we confess our sins, he is
faithful and just, and will forgive our sins and cleanse us
from all unrighteousness" (I John 1:9). So faith takes God
at His Word, believes it, and experiences forgiveness of
sins.

The Word of God says: "I am the resurrection and the
life; he who believes in me, though he die, yet shall he live"
(John 11:25). Faith takes God at His Word, discovers the
sting taken out of death, and finds new life in Christ.

The key, you see, is believing. The message of St. Paul to
the Philippian jailer speaks as directly to us today, if we will
only receive it:

"Believe in the Lord Jesus, and you will be saved"
(Acts 16:31).

This leads us to the third stage in the experience of this
young girl—the stage of voluntary service in love.

"Sir," she said to President Lincoln, "if it is true that I am
now free, and can go wherever I want, and do whatever I
wish, then I want to stay with you forever, and serve you
until I die."

Notice that the whole ground of their relationship had
shifted and the whole basis for service had changed. She

would have served him had he never set her free, but then
the service would have sprung from fear and force. Now
she wanted to serve him of her own free will, out of love
and gratitude.

Have you ever noticed what a difference motive makes
in the spirit and quality of a person's work? Not many of us
do our best work when we are forced against our will. One
of the wonderful things about our God is that He never
forces us to serve or obey Him. He invites us, rather, to
come to Him.

There is paradox in the service of Almighty God,
expressed in these words from *The Book of Common Prayer:*
"His service is perfect freedom." How is it that, in being
loosed from the bonds of sin and death, and binding ourselves in love as a slave to Jesus Christ, we can experience
perfect freedom? I don't know. It's the kind of truth that
cannot be explained; it can only be experienced.

As I look around the world at those people who are still
in bondage to sin and death, I affirm with the Word of God:
"Believe in the Lord Jesus, and you will be saved."

As I look around the Church, at those believers who
seem to have experienced deliverance from the bondage of
sin and death, and yet not discovered the joy and freedom
of serving Christ, to them I would offer the invitation of
our Lord Jesus:

> "Come to me, all who labor and are heavy-laden,
> and I will give you rest ... For my yoke is easy,
> and my burden is light" (Matthew 11:28, 30).

Remember, "If the Son makes you free, you will be free
indeed" (John 8:36).

How does one explain these things? I really do not know.
Perhaps the poet, Harry Webb Farrington, can express it
better than I:

I know not how that Bethlehem Babe
Could in the Godhead be;
I only know the Manger Child
Has brought God's life to me.

I know not how that Calvary's cross
A world from sin could free;
I only know its matchless love
Has brought God's love to me.

I know not how that Joseph's tomb
Could solve death's mystery;
I only know a living Christ,
Our Immortality.

VII

The Water of Life

"I Jesus have sent mine angel to testify unto these things in the churches. I am the root and the offspring of David, and the bright and morning star.

And the Spirit and the bride say, Come. And let him that is athirst come. And whosoever will, let him take the water of life freely" (Revelation 22:16, 17).

One of the best-known conversations recorded from ancient times—one that we alluded to briefly in Chapter Two—is a conversation Jesus had with a woman at a well in Samaria. John tells of this interview in the fourth chapter of his Gospel. He relates that Jesus had been in Judea, and that He wanted to go north into the province of Galilee.

Normally, a Jew traveling north from Judea to Galilee would go out of his way to avoid Samaria. He would travel down the Jericho Road, cross the Jordan River, head up the far side of the Jordan, then enter the land of Galilee somewhere near the south end of the Sea of Galilee.

But Jesus did not do this. Instead, He took the direct route—straight north through the land of Samaria.

About noon, Jesus came to Jacob's well in the town of Sychar—a well that had been a familiar watering spot and resting place for weary travelers for centuries. As Jesus rested by the well, a woman came along whom, in a most natural way, Jesus asked for a drink of water.

Far from reacting casually, however, she expressed surprise that He, a Jew, would ask a woman of Samaria for water. For as she pointed out, the Jews had no dealings with the Samaritans.

For us to understand why they didn't, it is necessary to go back in time more than 700 years prior to this conversation. At that time the city of Samaria, as capital of the northern kingdom of Israel, was conquered by the Assyrians, who took into captivity all the Jews who were young and strong and gifted. In their place, the Assyrians imported other conquered peoples to intermarry with the remaining Israelites.

Their purpose, of course, was to mix the population racially so that the Israelites would not mount any possible rebellion.

Over the centuries, the resulting mixed race of "Samaritans" established their own religious priesthood. Although Jewish Law stipulated that worship be offered at the Temple in Jerusalem, the Samaritans erected their own temple on Mount Gerizim. And they did not accept the whole of the Old Testament Scriptures; they accepted only the writings of Moses.

From a Jewish point of view, therefore, the Samaritans had a defective worship and a defective view of Scripture. Gradually over the centuries, an intense hostility grew up between the Jews and the Samaritans.

That being so, how dare Jesus tell a story one day in which a despised Samaritan emerged as the hero? (Tradition calls him the "Good Samaritan"; but from a

Jewish perspective that was a contradiction in terms! How in the world could you have a *good* Samaritan?)

You remember the story. A man traveling from Jerusalem to Jericho was beaten, robbed and left for dead beside the road. Along came a priest, and later a Levite, who both passed by on the other side. (Jesus did not say why neither helped the man in his obvious need. Perhaps they were hurrying on to a committee meeting in Jericho— one called to discuss the need to clean up the Jericho Road!)

In any case, the so-called "Good Samaritan," seeing the man who had been beaten and robbed, placed him on his own donkey, carried him to a nearby inn and offered to pay whatever it would cost to restore him to health.

Is it clear to you that Jesus did not share the petty prejudices of the people of His day? His response to the woman at the well, when she commented on His being a Jew and asking her for water, is interesting.

> "If you knew the gift of God, and who it is that is saying to you, 'Give me a drink,' you would have asked him, and he would have given you living water" (John 4:10).

The woman didn't understand what He was talking about.

> "Sir, you have nothing to draw with, and the well is very deep; where do you get that living water? Are you greater than our father Jacob, who gave us the well, and drank from it himself ... ?" (verses 11-12).

Jesus replied,

> "Every one who drinks of this water will thirst again, but whoever drinks of the water that I

shall give him will never thirst; the water that I
shall give him will become in him a spring of
water welling up to eternal life" (verses 13-14).

The Samaritan woman mistook Him to mean literal,
physical water; and that she would no longer need to come
to the well and draw. Jesus had begun, after all, by asking
for a drink. But the Lord had discerned in this woman a
great spiritual need and had changed the level of the conversation to refer to a deeper thirst than she was even
aware of.

We all know what it means to be thirsty, when to drink is
to satisfy that need. In the Bible, thirsting is used to teach
us something profoundly important about God. For
example, the psalmist wrote,

"As a hart longs for flowing streams, so longs my
soul for thee, O God. My soul thirsts for God, for
the living God" (Psalm 42:1-2).

The difference between this psalmist and the woman at
the well is only that he knew for whom he thirsted and she
did not.

It came out later in their conversation, however, when
Jesus told the woman to get her husband, and she
demurred that she had no husband.

Jesus responded,

"You are right in saying, 'I have no husband,' for
you have had five husbands, and he whom you
now have is not your husband; this you said
truly" (verses 17-18).

Perhaps you begin to recognize that this woman had a
deep and insatiable thirst that drove her from one casual

alliance to another. She yearned for the living God, just as the psalmist did, but Jesus alone knew it.

I am convinced St. Augustine was right when he said that God has a place within us—a "God-shaped vacuum," some call it. Try as we may to fill in any other way, that special place cannot be satisfied. You and I, you see, were made for God. We were made to be indwelt by His presence. And though we may try to satisfy this deep inner need by some other means, it never works.

What was the living water, then, that Jesus offered the Samaritan woman? What was it He said would satisfy perfectly the deep longing within her heart?

He spoke of it another time, this time before a crowd of people. John begins the story:

> "On the last day of the feast, the great day, Jesus stood up and proclaimed, 'If any one thirst, let him come to me and drink'"(John 7:37).

Most Bible scholars agree that the feast referred to here was the Feast of Tabernacles, one of the three great Jewish feasts that drew all able-bodied men within commuting distance to the city of Jerusalem. On the last day of that feast, the liturgy provided for several great earthenware jars of water placed just outside the gate of the Temple to be overturned before the crowd. As the water spilled out, the words from Psalm 42 were read about thirsting for God.

We may imagine, as this took place, that Jesus might have been standing within the Temple courtyard, perhaps in a distant corner, as He raised His voice:

> "If any one thirst, let him come to me and drink."

He assumed, of course, that if people did not thirst, they would not drink. So here we have a fundamental truth of

the Christian faith: our awareness of God usually arises
out of the recognition of some kind of inner need.

One of my best friends taught for some time at Harvard
Medical School and became a national authority on the
subject of suicide. He told me, having read many suicide
notes, that a common theme running through those notes
is a profound sense of purposelessness. "Life has no
meaning," they write. "There's no reason to go on."

For other people, a crushing sense of guilt may open
their eyes to their need for God.

But whatever needs an individual may experience, it is
much the same with the Gospel as it is with Alcoholics
Anonymous. Until and unless a person acknowledges his
alcoholism, there is nothing A.A. can do for him. So in the
Christian life, until we are prepared to acknowledge that
we have a need before God, there is nothing He can do for
us.

It is to the person who recognizes his thirst—though he
may not know how to satisfy that thirst—that Jesus says,
"Let him come to me and drink."

What an extraordinary invitation! The prophets never
talked that way. They said, in effect, "Turn to the Lord and
He will heal you." Jesus said, "Come to me, all who labor
and are heavy-laden, and I will give you rest" (Matthew
11:28).

Jesus claimed in Himself the ability to satisfy the deepest
hunger and thirst of the human heart. He called Himself
the bread of heaven. He offered the gift of living water.
And He spoke of the necessity of eating His flesh and
drinking His blood.

Would you agree that you could stand on the bank of a
fast-flowing stream of clear, cool water and die of thirst?
Would you agree that you could stand beside a banqueting
table laden with rich food and die of starvation? You can be
in the presence of what can satisfy your need, and still not
receive it.

So it was that Jesus said to the crowd at the Feast of Tabernacles, "If any one thirst, let him come to me and drink." What does it mean to drink? It means to receive into yourself what you need to satisfy that seemingly insatiable thirst within you.

Jesus continued, painting a glorious word-picture:

> "He who believes in me, as the scripture has said,
> 'Out of his heart shall flow rivers of living
> water'" (John 7:38).

Do you see the picture? Jesus was addressing the thirst of the human heart. He had said to the woman at the well, "The water that I shall give him will become in him a spring of water welling up to eternal life." He now declared to the crowd in Jerusalem, referring to anyone who believed in Him, "Out of his heart shall flow rivers of living water." And He says the same to us today:

> "Let him who is thirsty come, let him who desires
> take the water of life without price" (Revelation
> 22:17).

Can you see it's a matter of receiving something into our lives that, once present, becomes an artesian well flowing out of us?

This "something" is very simple. John articulated plainly what the living water Jesus spoke of is.

> "Now this [Jesus] said about the Spirit, which
> those who believed in him were to receive; for as
> yet the Spirit had not been given, because Jesus
> was not yet glorified" (John 7:39).

You and I were created to be filled with the Spirit of God. The water of life that Jesus offers this weary world is none

other than God Himself in the fullness of His Holy Spirit.
St. Paul wrote of this living water to the Corinthians:

> "For by one Spirit we were all baptized into one
> body—Jews or Greeks, slaves or free—and all
> were made to drink of one Spirit" (I Corinthians
> 12:13).

The Spirit of God, then, is the *gift* of God to those who
believe in Jesus Christ. And when the Spirit of God comes
to indwell our lives, He is like living water given to us—
water that cleanses, refreshes, renews, overflows, and
brings blessing wherever we go.

Some years ago, just before the revolution in Iran, I was
invited by the Anglican bishop of Iran, the Rt. Rev. B.
Dehqani-Tafti, to present a series of "missions" throughout that country. One day I was flying from Tehran down
to Shiraz in the southern part of the country.

I remember being impressed, as we flew over the land, at
the barrenness below. There was, as far as I could see,
nothing but endless desert—no vegetation, or roads, or
any signs of civilization at all.

Then, out of the corner of my eye, I saw a spot on the
sand up ahead. As we flew closer, I could see that it was
completely square and appeared, at that distance, to be
black.

I knew it was no natural phenomenon. So I asked the
flight attendant about it.

"That is an experiment of our government," she smiled.
"Our government was drilling for oil in the desert, but
they didn't find oil. Instead, they struck an artesian well of
water. They capped the well, laid pipe across the sand for a
distance of one square mile, and regulated the flow of
water to just a tiny mist. What you see now is what
happened when the water began to flow over the sand.
Before a month had passed, little shoots of green began to

appear on the sand. Now it's a veritable jungle, one square mile of it. Nothing was ever planted. The only thing that made the difference was water."

I marveled, sitting there on the plane that day, as I considered the inescapable reality: it takes water to produce life. And in the supernatural realm, it takes God's Spirit to produce spiritual life. The Holy Spirit is God's water of life to be shed abroad in our lives.

We live in a dry world. People are desperately thirsting for what will bring cleansing renewal and new life to them. You and I, who know the Lord Jesus and have been filled with His Holy Spirit, are artesian wells. Out of us flows day by day a stream of life and blessing, touching all the people with whom we come in contact, bringing life and light and cleansing and joy and refreshment.

So it was that, although Jesus asked the woman at the well for a drink of water, before long He was speaking of that which would satisfy the deepest thirst of *her* heart.

I have a question for you. Have you received the gift of the Holy Spirit? This is Jesus' first gift to us. When we come to Him and receive what He offers us, it is like drinking a glass of cool, refreshing water. And that water is the Holy Spirit.

God wants to fill our lives with Himself! He wants us to be full-to-overflowing with His own life, because that is what will bring blessing and refreshment to this troubled world.

Father in heaven, we thank You for the gracious provision of new life through Jesus Christ. We thank You for the gift of Your Holy Spirit, to shed abroad in our hearts light, refreshment, and cleansing. Move upon each of us, that we may hear with joy, and receive with faithfulness, the gift You offer us. And grant that our lives may be so filled with Your Spirit, that they may overflow and bring refreshment wherever we go. Grant it for Jesus' sake, we pray. Amen.

VIII

Lessons From Cracked Pots

"The word which came to Jeremiah from the Lord, saying,
Arise, and go down to the potter's house, and there I will cause thee to hear my words.
Then I went down to the potter's house, and, behold, he wrought a work on the wheels.
And the vessel that he made of clay was marred in the hand of the potter: so he made it again another vessel, as seemed good to the potter to make it.
Then the word of the Lord came to me, saying,
O house of Israel, cannot I do with you as this potter? saith the Lord. Behold, as the clay is in the potter's hand, so are ye in mine hand, O house of Israel" (Jeremiah 18:1-6).

The prophet Jeremiah tells of a strange and fascinating experience that occurred in his ministry to Judah and Jerusalem just before those proud people were taken into captivity by their Babylonian conquerors.
He describes how one day the word of the Lord came to

him, instructing him to go into the city of Jerusalem to buy a clay pot—an earthen vessel. He was then told to take some of the elders of the people and some of the senior priests, and accompany them to the gate of Jerusalem. There he was to preach a message from the Lord.

That message was startling; it began like this:

> "Thus says the Lord of hosts, the God of Israel, Behold, I am bringing such evil upon this place that the ears of every one who hears of it will tingle. Because the people have forsaken me, and have profaned this place by burning incense in it to other gods whom neither they nor their fathers nor the kings of Judah have known; and because they have filled this place with the blood of innocents, and have built the high places of Baal to burn their sons in the fire as burnt offerings to Baal, which I did not command or decree, nor did it come into my mind; therefore, behold, days are coming, says the Lord, when this place shall no more be called Topheth, or the Valley of Benhinnom, but the Valley of Slaughter" (Jeremiah 19:3-6).

To Jeremiah God gave this additional word of instruction:

> "Then you shall break the flask in the sight of the men who go with you, and shall say to them, Thus says the Lord of hosts: So will I break this people and this city, as one breaks a potter's vessel, so that it can never be mended" (verses 10-11).

Jeremiah was being commanded by the Lord not only to preach a message of judgment and imminent destruction upon the people because of their idolatry and faithlessness. He was also being commanded to act that message out symbolically before their very eyes. He was to take the clay pot he had purchased in the city and smash it on the ground, breaking it into a thousand pieces so it could never be mended.

Here we have it, then: a clay pot—an earthen vessel—broken in judgment as a symbol of the wrath of God against the sin and rebellion of His people.

In the New Testament, we find another story of a broken vessel, this one broken for another reason.

It took place just before the Passover as the chief priests and scribes plotted how they could do away with Jesus secretly to avoid making a stir.

> "While [Jesus] was at Bethany in the house of Simon the leper, as he sat at table, a woman came with an alabaster jar of ointment of pure nard, very costly, and she broke the jar and poured it over his head. But there were some who said to themselves indignantly, 'Why was the ointment thus wasted? For this ointment might have been sold for more than three hundred denarii, and given to the poor.' And they reproached her. But Jesus said, 'Let her alone; why do you trouble her? She has done a beautiful thing to me. For you always have the poor with you, and whenever you will, you can do good to them; but you will not always have me'" (Mark 14:3-7).

The vessel in this account was broken in sacrifice—as a symbol of a woman's love.

When we reflect on these two records side by side, we can see certain similarities and certain differences between them. In both, we have the account of a broken vessel—one broken in judgment and the other in love.

But this is not the only similarity. Both symbolic acts also speak of imminent death and judgment.

In Jeremiah's account, it was to be the death of the people because of their rebellion and sin. God declared through the prophet:

> "And in this place I will make void the plans of
> Judah and Jerusalem and will cause their people
> to fall by the sword before their enemies, and by
> the hand of those who seek their life" (Jeremiah
> 19:7).

History reveals that this prophecy was fulfilled when the Babylonians swept down upon Judah, destroyed Solomon's Temple that had stood for over 300 years, and killed multitudes of people. Jeremiah's act of breaking the vessel on the ground symbolized imminent death soon to come upon the people because of their sin before the Lord.

The same is true, though not as obvious, in the New Testament example. Here, Jesus explains the significance of the woman's sacrificial act to those who stood by and criticized. "She has done what she could; she has anointed my body beforehand for burying" (Mark 14:8).

A third similarity tying these two events together is that both occurred as a harbinger of divine judgment.

This is obvious in the case of Jeremiah; his message was clearly one of judgment on the people for their sin. It is equally true in the account of the woman and her broken alabaster jar of ointment.

In the New Testament, it was not the judgment of God on His people, but rather on His own Son. Jesus bore on the cross the judgment and wrath of Almighty God against the sin of the human race. The cross, for the Jew, represented not an object of beauty but a sign of divine judgment; for the Law taught that anyone who hung upon a cross fell under the judgment of God.

Isaiah, in prophesying about the coming Messiah and especially about His death, said:

> "Yet it was the will of the Lord to bruise him; he has put him to grief; when he makes himself an offering for sin... (Isaiah 53:10).

Jesus Christ, when He hung between heaven and earth, bore in His body the judgment of Almighty God for your sin and mine. Jesus became the Lamb of God who took away the sins of the world.

However striking the similarities between these two stories are, their dissimilarities are even more striking. I mention only two.

The most obvious, to me, is in what is symbolized. In Jeremiah, the vessel was broken as a symbol of judgment; whereas for the woman, the broken vessel symbolized sacrifice and love.

The broken alabaster jar of ointment was a symbol of sacrifice because it was costly. The Gospel writer makes a point of saying it was worth more than 300 denarii—about one year's wage for a working man of that day. Perhaps it had been a family heirloom passed down carefully from generation to generation. Never before had an occasion arisen that seemed significant enough to use it.

Now, however, with the approaching death of the One this woman had come to regard as her Lord and Savior, she broke it willingly. As the fragrance filled the room, it spoke to everyone of the love she bore for her Lord Jesus Christ.

So there you have it: two jars broken, one in judgment, and one in love. But perhaps you are wondering what this has to do with you or me.

The answer is that our lives will be characterized ultimately by one or the other of these two jars. Which one will depend on us.

The Bible expresses our present relationship to God metaphorically in a number of ways: the Lord is the shepherd, we are the sheep; He is our Father, we are His children; He is the vine, we are the branches.

Another expression of our relationship common to both Old and New Testaments is that God is the potter and we are the clay. Here is just one Old Testament example:

> "Yet, O Lord, thou art our Father; we are the
> clay, and thou art our potter; we are all the work
> of thy hand" (Isaiah 64:8).

In thinking about this Biblical metaphor, one could arrive at a false conclusion. Since clay is a lifeless and inert substance, molded at the will of the potter, one might get the idea that man is simply a passive agent who is acted upon in life and that God will ultimately shape him any way He likes.

Many people, including some Christian theologians, have interpreted man's relationship to God in just this fatalistic way—as though man had no part in the shaping of his destiny.

This, of course, is nonsense. Any such interpretation of our relationship with God that disregards our autonomy is simply false.

One of the most wonderful, and also the most terrifying, aspects of man's nature is that he really is free. He is not simply a blob in the hands of God to be shaped this way or that. God has not created a race of marionettes manipulated by some invisible strings. Nor has He created a line-up of automatons to be controlled by the push of a button.

Because God has given freedom to man, man is the only creature who can turn around and spit in the face of God; he is the only creature who can resist his destiny; he is the only creature who can take his life into his own hands and try to shape it according to his own desires and plans; he is the only creature who can stamp his foot and shake his fist at God and say no. And man is the only creature with the freedom to ruin his own life and the lives of those around him.

This is precisely the point I am getting at. God is indeed like a potter. Our lives are indeed like clay in His hands. God desires to mold and fashion each of us into vessels of beauty and usefulness. But the accomplishment of this objective is not automatic; *it requires our cooperation.*

The question of our achieving a life of beauty and usefulness does not depend upon how many talents we have, or what kind of circumstances surround our lives. There are people with ten talents, of course, and some with only one. There are people who, because of favorable circumstances, have been able to go farther in life than others.

But the question of our beauty or usefulness does not turn on either our native abilities or our circumstances. It depends upon our will; it is a matter of commitment.

One of the amazing things we read in the Scriptures is that we are called on to become co-laborers with God. We can enter into partnership with God simply by offering our lives to Him.

Jesus said that anyone who came to Him would never be turned away. There is no possibility that we could offer our life to Christ and have it turned down; the altar sanctifies the gift. If we give ourselves to Christ, we may be sure He will accept us, and begin to mold and fashion and shape our lives according to His perfect will.

When we reach the end of our lives, I wonder which of the two images we have read about in Scripture will best describe us. Will we be vessels whose lives have been broken and fractured into a thousand pieces that can never be mended? Or will we be a broken jar of ointment—giving off a fragrance to everyone around—that speaks of a life lived to the glory of Almighty God?

Whatever our answer, I am sure of one thing. Whether our lives become vessels of beauty and usefulness, or vessels broken utterly beyond repair, depends not only on the power and will of Almighty God, but on how we ourselves have responded to Christ's invitation to be clay in the Potter's hand.

> *Have Thine own way, Lord, have Thine own way,*
> *Thou art the Potter, we are the clay;*
> *Mold us and make us after Thy will,*
> *While we are waiting, yielded and still.*
>
> *Amen.*

IX

Conversion: A Must or A Maybe?

"Knowing, brethren beloved, your election [is] of God. For our gospel came not unto you in word only, but also in power, and in the Holy Ghost, and in much assurance; as ye know what manner of men we were among you for your sake.

For from you sounded out the word of the Lord not only in Macedonia and Achaia, but also in every place your faith to God-ward is spread abroad; so that we need not to speak any thing.

For they themselves show of us what manner of entering in we had unto you, and how ye turned to God from idols to serve the living and true God"

(I Thessalonians 1:4-5, 8-9).

Forty days after our Lord's resurrection, He stood on the summit of the Mount of Olives, that scraggly little elevation just outside Jerusalem, surrounded by His eleven disciples.

In those last, solemn moments before His ascension and return to the Father, He turned to His disciples and uttered those words we have come to call "the Great Commission." This is the charge that defines, for all time, the purpose and sets the task of the Christian Church:

> "All authority in heaven and on earth has been given to me. Go therefore and make disciples of all nations, baptizing them in the name of the Father and of the Son and of the Holy Spirit, teaching them to observe all that I have commanded you; and lo, I am with you always, to the close of the age" (Matthew 28:18-20).

After speaking these words, our Lord was caught up from among them and was soon lost to their sight. The disciples, according to Luke's Gospel, then turned from that sacred spot, descended the mountain, and returned to Jerusalem with joy in their hearts and the words of the Great Commission ringing in their ears.

To these first Christians, Jesus had made it unmistakably clear that the first task of the Church was to make disciples from among all nations, baptizing them in the name of the Father and of the Son and of the Holy Spirit, and teaching them all that they had been taught by Jesus Himself.

These early Christians went everywhere bearing witness to Jesus Christ by their transformed lives and by the words of their lips, calling men to repentance of sin and to faith in Christ. These Christians were out to make converts!

Conversion looms large in New Testament thought. To present Christ in such a way as to elicit faith in Him was the aim and purpose of apostolic preaching. The early church was made up of people who had been changed by the power of God and went about everywhere proclaiming the transforming message of the Gospel.

They were themselves converted, transformed, changed. They spoke as converts, they wrote as converts, and they lived as converts. They knew something had happened to them. The entrance of Christ into their lives had made all things new.

They could say with the man who was born blind, "Though I was blind, now I see" (John 9:25). They had been transformed by Jesus Christ, and it was this experience, together with Jesus' assurance that He would be with them even to the end of the age, that sent them out as flaming evangelists to change the world.

In this section, I want to expand our discussion of the first two chapters and look at the experience of conversion. What does it mean, anyway?

St. Paul was speaking of conversion when he wrote:

"Put off your old nature which belongs to your former manner of life and is corrupt through deceitful lusts... and put on the new nature, created after the likeness of God in true righteousness and holiness" (Ephesians 4:22, 24).

In this Scripture, and in many others, we find that conversion means turning our back on our former way of life; putting off our old nature with its sins and lusts; and putting on a new nature that is God's creation, one that results in a righteous and holy life.

Conversion is an about-face, a turning around of our loyalties, a reversal of our values, a bisection of our life into a "B.C." and an "A.D.," a "before" and an "after." It is as St. Paul wrote:

"...if any one is in Christ, he is a new creation;
the old has passed away, behold, the new has
come" (II Corinthians 5:17).

The word *conversion* is used only once in the New Testament (in Acts 15:3), but the verb *convert* is used more often. Literally, it means "to turn about."

Biblically speaking, conversion describes the initial coming to God in Jesus Christ, when a person becomes a Christian in conscious and personal experience. It implies a coming alive to God through Christ; the act of being recognized to God.

It is the state of soul when a person declares from his heart, "Abba, Father," because he has now been adopted into sonship. It is that glad and glorious freedom, the realization of a radical new start, in which a person knows he has the right to call himself, humbly and yet truly, a child of God. A converted person has passed a landmark in his spiritual experience.

This experience came in mid-life to the great Russian novelist, Leo Tolstoy.

"Five years ago," he wrote, "I came to believe in Christ, and my life suddenly began to change. I ceased to desire what I had previously desired and began to desire what I formerly did not want. What previously seemed to me good seemed evil; and what seemed evil seemed good. It happened to me as it happens to a man who goes out on some business and on the way suddenly decides that the business is unnecessary and returns home. All that was on his right is now on his left, and all that was on his left is now on his right. The former wish, to get as far as possible from home, has changed into a wish to be as near as possible to it. The direction of my life and my desires became different, and good and evil changed places."

For this man, conversion resulted in a clear-cut change of direction, a passing away of the former life and the discovery of a new life. Tolstoy had become a new creation in Christ Jesus.

On Jesus' ascension day, He sent His disciples out to evangelize the world with the message of forgiveness of sins and peace with God through faith in Jesus Christ. This command of our Lord has never been revoked.

I am impressed by the definition of evangelism given by the great Anglican Archbishop of Canterbury, William Temple.

To evangelize, he said, is "so to present Christ Jesus in the power of the Holy Spirit that men shall come to put their trust in God through Him, to accept Him as their Savior, and to serve Him as their King in the fellowship of the Church."

I like this definition because it has a New Testament ring about it!

In his book *The Practice of Evangelism*, Canon Bryan Green devotes a chapter to what he calls "The Necessity of Conversion," in which he puts the matter this way:

"This is the object that we have in view when we seek to evangelize—to bring men into true conversion. By pre-evangelism, we seek to awaken them to their need of God's salvation through Christ. In evangelism, we present Christ to them by the Spirit with the definite aim to convert them. After conversion they need pastoral care with the fellowship of the Church, with the opportunity for worship and service."

I can almost sense the quesions that may be arising in some of your minds, if you have been reading carefully. Some of you may be thinking that you have never had any such dramatic experience as Tolstoy describes; and you may be wondering if Bryan Green is trying to say that only people who have had these experiences are real Christians. Others of you may be thinking, "Did I not become a Christian when I was baptized?"

To answer these important questions, let's first explore

the connection between conversion and the Christian life. And in order to do this we must ask one additional question: What *is* a Christian?

This is a big question. Too simple an answer may be misleading. Fundamentally, however, it is a matter of relationship. *A Christian is a person who has entered a new relationship with God through faith in the Lord Jesus Christ, and into a new relationship with God's people, the Church, through baptism.*

For those of you who may accept or emphasize only half this definition, to the neglect of the other half (whichever that happens to be), stay with me! Let's look at both sides together, and see if we can't arrive at a balanced view.

Becoming a Christian in the full New Testament sense includes both a vertical and a horizontal dimension. That is to say, it has to do with belonging both to God and to the Church. *Faith* initiates the first of these relationships, *baptism* the second.

It is by faith that we accept the salvation of God freely offered to us in the cross of our Lord Jesus Christ; and it is through baptism that we are incorporated into that society of people who bear Christ's name and who form the outward and visible Church.

"He who believes and is baptized," Jesus said, "will be saved" (Mark 16:16). So a Christian, as the New Testament teaches it, is a person who has entered into both these relationships.

Let's look at the "believing" or faith side of the coin first. Faith, in the Biblical sense, is not simply believing God in a general sort of way. One could believe in Jesus as one believes in Napoleon, as a historical figure (although, so far as I know, that will do nothing for you). Rather, faith involves personal trust in the Lord Jesus—not merely intellectual assent, but personal commitment to Him as Savior and Master.

This is what Jesus was saying to Nicodemus—as we saw

in Chapter Six—when He said, "You must be born anew."
This is what it means to believe.

Do you believe? Have you a personal faith in Jesus
Christ? That is the all-important issue; for it is only by
faith in Jesus that we lay hold on all that God has done for
us in the cross of His Son. It is only by faith that we receive
the forgiveness of our sins and become the children of
God.

A familiar verse in the New Testament puts it this way:

> "But to all who received him, who believed in his
> name, he gave power to become children of God"
> (John 1:12).

What has conversion to do with all this? We must
remember, the first Christians had previously been either
pagans or Jews. When these people came into a new
relationship with God through faith in Christ, it meant a
radical about-face, the crossing of a clear line of demar-
cation, a separation of the Christian from the non-
Christian.

Conversion to Christ often meant even the forsaking of
family and friends; so that the price of this new-found faith
was high indeed. In those early days of Christianity, a
person knew whether he was a Christian or not because
conversion cost something.

This is still true in those parts of the world where Christ
is being preached for the first time. In these situations, to
convert is to take a stand for Jesus against many threaten-
ing odds. These people know they are Christians; and,
what is more, other people knew it, too.

In the early days of the Christian Church, the converts
were baptized immediately as a sign of their newfound
faith. This sacrament of water baptism represents the
other half of the conversion coin.

Baptism became the outward sign of the inward work of regeneration. It symbolized identification with Jesus in death and burial. And it represented the new convert's obedience to Jesus' clear word of command.

These early Christians, moreover, wanted their children to be brought up differently than they themselves had been. So the Church faced the question of how to regard the children of believing parents. Were they to be considered pagans and outsiders until they became old enough to choose Christ for themselves?

The earliest Christians said no. Persuaded, rather, of the good will of our God toward the children of believing parents, they began the practice very early of baptizing them, and so bringing them into the fellowship of God's family, the Church. It can even be looked at as the fulfillment of the Old Testament rite of circumcision.

Baptism was not the end of the Church's responsibility, of course. It was only the beginning! Jesus had commanded His followers to go out into all the world and make disciples, baptizing them in the name of the Father and the Son and the Holy Spirit, and teaching them all that He had commanded them.

It was the responsibility of Christian parents, therefore, and indeed of the whole Church, to see that the individuals being baptized (whether adults or children), were taught all things necessary to their souls' health and nurtured in their personal faith.

There are many today who continue that early practice of baptizing their children. Others regard baptism as a sign, once a person is old enough, that he has chosen to embrace the faith for himself. Both points of view agree that a Christian is one who has come into a new relationship with God through faith in Christ, and with the Church through baptism. They simply differ on which comes first.

Those who practice "believers' baptism" say that a

person should first enter a new relationship with God by faith in Christ, and only secondly be baptized into the Church of Christ as a public witness of his faith. These people are sometimes said to espouse "adult" baptism (as opposed to "infant" baptism).

But this is the wrong way to put it. In fact, they believe a person must know in his heart that he is a child of God through faith in Christ before he can be baptized; so their preaching aims at bringing a person to conversion. Only after the person has responded in some visible way—perhaps by raising his hand or walking down the aisle—is he considered a candidate for baptism.

Other churches believe a child may be baptized first and brought under the care of the Church, being trained in the faith until he comes to the place of personal commitment later on. These churches concentrate not so much on bringing people to conversion as on the more gradual method of teaching and training.

Because the word *disciple* means "learner," these churches follow almost literally the words of the Great Commission: "Go therefore and make disciples [or learners] of all nations," [by] "baptizing them in the name of the Father and of the Son and of the Holy Spirit, teaching them to observe all that I have commanded you." Baptize them first, then teach them.

Both points of view can get sidetracked. On the one hand, certain believers place so much stress on securing a vertical relationship with God through Christ that the Church may seem superfluous (when, in fact, the Bible knows nothing of unbaptized or "lone ranger" Christians).

Certain other believers, once having baptized a child and called him by Christ's name, over-emphasize the horizontal relationship with the Church and assume that alone is sufficient.

Both these positions, however widespread in the Church, distort the truth as Jesus Himself gave it to us.

"He who believes *and* is baptized," He said, "will be saved" (italics mine).

It may be that someone reading these words has been baptized, and even nurtured by the Church, but has never put personal faith in Jesus Christ. (Such a conversion need not be so dramatic a turn-around as that of Leo Tolstoy to be genuine.)

If you have not invited Jesus into your life, then according to the New Testament you are a Christian in name only. An account in the Bank of Heaven has been opened for you, but you have not yet drawn on the infinite riches of the grace of God deposited there.

To you I quote the words of the Lord Jesus:

> "For this is the will of my Father, that every one who sees the Son and believes in him should have eternal life; and I will raise him up at the last day" (John 6:40).

There may be someone else reading this who knows he is a Christian by personal faith in Christ, but who has never been baptized or become part of Christ's universal Church. To you I quote the words of Peter on the Day of Pentecost:

> "Repent, and be baptized every one of you" (Acts 2:38).

Believing and being baptized are both part of what it means to become a Christian. Our God is calling each one of us to become a Christian in fact as well as in name. He is calling on us to believe in the Lord Jesus Christ; to receive Him by faith into our lives, that He may be Lord of our lives.

And God is calling us into the fellowship of His Church

through baptism, to be joined with other Christians in the Body of Christ.

How have you responded to both these calls? Let God's Word speak to your heart.

Father in heaven, who by the power of Your Holy Spirit sent forth Your apostles to make disciples of all nations baptizing them into Your Church, quicken, we ask You, by the same Spirit, the Church of these latter days. With wisdom and zeal may we preach Your Gospel to those who dwell in darkness, till all men everywhere are brought into the clear light and true knowledge of You and Your Son, Jesus Christ our Lord. Amen.

X

A Sight to Make Hell Tremble

"And I saw an angel come down from heaven, having the key of the bottomless pit and a great chain in his hand.

And he laid hold on the dragon, that old serpent, which is the Devil, and Satan, and bound him a thousand years,

And cast him into the bottomless pit, and shut him up, and set a seal upon him, that he should deceive the nations no more, till the thousand years should be fulfilled: and after that he must be loosed a little season.

And I saw thrones, and they sat upon them, and judgment was given unto them: and I saw the souls of them that were beheaded for the witness of Jesus and for the word of God, and which had not worshipped the beast, neither his image, neither had received his mark upon their foreheads, or in their hands; and they lived and reigned with Christ a thousand years.

But the rest of the dead lived not again until the thousand years were finished. This is the first resurrection.

Blessed and holy is he that hath part in the first resurrection: on such the second death hath no power, but

they shall be priests of God and of Christ, and shall reign
with him a thousand years"   (Revelation 20: 1-6).

In C. S. Lewis' wonderfully "diabolical" little book, *The Screwtape Letters,* we find a senior devil writing advice to one of his subordinates, who has been assigned the task of keeping a certain man "out of the Enemy's clutches"—meaning God.

When the "patient" becomes a Christian, the junior tempter gets worried. But Screwtape reassures him that he may have nothing to worry about. And he proceeds to recommend the technique of so absorbing the patient with the idiosyncrasies and defects of his fellow believers, especially in church, that he will become convinced that their own religion is mere hypocrisy or convention.

Screwtape prefaces his suggestion by stating that one of hell's greatest allies in preventing the patient from advancing in his Christian faith is the Church. But he pauses for a moment.

"Do not misunderstand me," he says. "I do not mean the Church as we see her spread out through all time and space and rooted in eternity, terrible as an army with banners. That, I confess, is a spectacle which makes our boldest tempters uneasy. But fortunately it is quite invisible to these humans."

It is hard to imagine a more vivid picture than that of the Christian Church with all its banners flying, striking fear into the hosts of hell!

While all of us may appreciate so graphic a picture, however, we might well ask, when we look from the picture to the facts, whether Lewis did not overstate the case. It is difficult to observe the Church as it is today and understand how it could possibly constitute much of a threat to the kingdom of darkness.

Within and without, critics have exposed mercilessly the

petty bickerings, the irrelevant preaching, the indifferent living that goes on within the many expressions of the Church universal. Far from being an army on the offensive for Jesus Christ and seeking to subdue the strongholds of evil, the Church has been placed on the defensive.

Some critics consider the Church to have degenerated beyond reclaim. These people are saying that the old ways of thinking, the old moral codes, and the old conceptions of theology have become bankrupt; and that God Himself, if we were only awake enough to see it, is foreclosing on the whole deal.

Others are prepared to give up on the very idea of "God" as simply a word with so many meanings as to be of no use whatever in religious communication. These theologians speak boldly of the "death of God," and call for a new theology, a theology for the secular city, or a theology for a world that has come of age.

The Church has its critics; their number is legion. And personally, I am convinced that much of their criticism is utterly deserved, and that we who love the Church would do well to take heed.

It is not my purpose in this chapter, however, to join these critics and call for the demise of the Church. You see, I stand within the Church—not only my particular denomination, the Episcopal Church, but every expression of the Church of Jesus Christ all over the world. Its weaknesses are my weaknesses. Its strengths are my strengths.

I long for the Church at its best: not on the defensive against the fiery attacks within and without, but squarely on the offensive for Jesus Christ, with all its banners flying, causing the very ruler of hell to quail.

In this chapter, I would like to look with you at four variations of hell at work in our society, all of which are included in Jesus' promise:

"The gates of hell shall not prevail against [my
Church]" (Matthew 16:18).

Jesus' triumph over the first expression of hell—the
literal realm of darkness ruled by the devil and his hosts—
is symbolized for me in one of the great photographs of the
century. It appeared in *Life* magazine in an article on the
Vietnam War. The picture, in full color, showed an
American soldier lying face down on the ground, dead. In
that one figure was gathered the whole meaning of the
cost of that terrible war. It was the price of advance into
enemy territory.

The cross, which stands forever at the center of the
Church, is our reminder of the awful price Jesus paid to
regain the territory usurped by Satan. Jesus entered the
earthly realm where sin held men in its grip. He conquered
sin by destroying its power, and defeated even our last
enemy, death, by His mighty resurrection.

Today, although the enemy still occupies the territory in
which we live, the Church possesses the living power of
the resurrection. The same power that conquered sin and
death pulsates at the heart of the Church through the
power of the risen Christ.

And if the Church becomes what Jesus intended it to
be—a resurrection society—then hell has reason to
tremble. For here is a force adequate to hold back the over-
whelming tide of evil and topple its princes: a power won at
a supreme price. The Church, with the crucified and risen
Lord as its Head, is witness to both the price and the power.

People living in the power of Christ's victory are "new"
people; and the place you find the power to be born anew is
the Church.

After the resurrection, Jesus made His disciples new
creatures one by one—Peter, Thomas, the two on their
way to Emmaus. But it was in the company of believers,

who were together in one place, that the power of God fell on that first Pentecost and the Church was born.

Today, too, the power of God is seen and felt most clearly among small groups of people who earnestly seek to grow in grace through the study of the Scriptures, through prayer and through Christian fellowship.

You may argue that this power is often seen outside the Church. I will not deny it. But it always comes as an overflow from the Church; and unless it leads back into the Church, it will shrivel and die.

This power will die not only when it is cut off from the Church. It can die within the Church, too, whenever a local congregation becomes a country club, or little more than a reflection of the lives that come in through its doors.

The record of the Church has been blotted with failures down through the centuries. But those failures have never destroyed the resurrection power that Jesus has given, not only to individual Christians, but to His Church.

That mysterious and supernatural power has nerved the Church throughout the heroic days of its history: enduring persecution from governing powers; meeting the costly challenge of the missionary advance; mounting campaigns against slavery and exploitation; the confessional churches standing courageously against Nazi idolatry as every other voice and witness faded out.

Any body of believers that acknowledges the living Christ wields a power that does not flinch before evil's towering assaults. No wonder hell trembles at the sight of a Church whose banners have been raised by sinners who have been forgiven and are being transformed by the power of Jesus Christ in their midst!

Let's look at hell from a second perspective. A character in T. S. Eliot's "The Cocktail Party" put it this way: "Hell is oneself. Hell is alone, the other figures in it merely projections. There is nothing to escape from and nothing to escape to. One is always alone."

And read the words of William Morris, English poet of the last century: "Fellowship is life; lack of fellowship is hell."

It seems to be part of the strategy of the devil to keep people separated from one another in a hell of isolation, relating their lives to each other only superficially. We might wonder if the devil has not succeeded in promoting modern man's "individualism."

Life has become fractured, atomized. We are alone. Our hearts can break; we can even die, and the faceless people in the next apartment not even know, much less care.

This is a hell of a very different kind. One person alone is no match for powerful armies, whether they be the armies of entrenched evil, or the armies of the powers of darkness in our own souls. Even great masses of separate individuals cannot withstand the kingdom of hell on the march.

But imagine what it would be like if the walls between individuals were broken down and our separation overcome. Just suppose, somehow, that these atomized masses turned into people whose hearts and hands were joined in one communion, bound together by one Spirit.

Then, I say, hell had better tremble!

Jesus said, "Where two or three are gathered in my name, there am I in the midst of them" (Matthew 18:20). This kind of communion shakes hell to its core, because it drives the sword into the heart of despair (which is hell at its worst), and despair has no dominion over a communion of believers.

I have seen men and women struggling as best they could to cope with the complexities of life by themselves, but galvanized into new people by the Holy Spirit at work in a local fellowship that draws strength from its members and from the Lord.

Stand with me for a moment on the steps of an

imaginary church, as we watch the congregation assemble for worship. Let's assume we know most of the parishioners well. One by one they walk up the steps and through the door—a pretty sorry bunch of folks, really! Weak men and women, some of them spineless in character, others full of problems or inconsistencies.

As we follow them into the sanctuary, we see a sad assembly indeed! It is as mathematics teaches—that the whole is equal to the sum of its parts.

But let these people—flawed, ordinary—dare to invite Christ in the person of His Holy Spirit into their midst, and we suddenly observe more than a collection of frail men and women gathered in the room.

We find communion, fellowship, an antidote for their aloneness that has transformed them into something more than they were. An invisible plus has been added—a plus in the shape of a cross.

It is from the brokenness of Christ on the cross that we find healing for our aloneness, our separation. Is it any wonder that a Church like this strikes fear into the heart of hell?

A third view of hell is visible wherever people live with their eyes on the clock and on the ground, prisoners of time and space. It is good devilish strategy to keep a person's attention focused on petty annoyances; to make him behave as though he were nothing but a clod of ailments.

People who live in this hell get up in the morning and go to work, to earn some money to buy some bread, to gain the strength to get up in the morning and go to work, to earn some money to buy some bread, on and on in a dreary round of existence.

The devil wants men and women to think of life as a prisonhouse of time and space, the true homeland of their souls, the very antechamber of hell itself. Then the human race can wither itself away with no transfusion of life from beyond itself, no blessing or benediction from above.

Tramp the treadmill, eyes on the ground, until life burns out like a candle.

But let a person enter a church and start to worship with other people in the fellowship of the Holy Spirit; let him fling his soul upward to the heights; and then hell begins to tremble!

Men at worship are men at the threshold of discovering that the true homeland of their souls is not in the frantic round of *busyness*; that they are more than clods of ailments; that life has a dimension neither clock nor yardstick can show.

This is one great gift of Christ through the Church: the experience of pointing and lifting the soul toward God, above the anxiety and petty concerns of life.

Dorothy Wadsworth once wrote in her journal about Grasmere, her home in the lake country of England: "Very solemn in the last glimpses of twilight, it calls home the heart to quietness."

This is also a great ministry of the Church. A believing community of faith; the reading of the Word; music; preaching; the familiar appointments of altar, cross, candles—all these call home the heart to quietness, to self-transcendence. The reminder that we are not prisoners of time and space is the gift of the Church at worship.

Ola Winslow, in her book on colonial New England, tells how these sturdy people built a church at the center of each village, symbolic of the vital center of their lives.

"Somehow it embodied fundamental loyalties," she writes, "and created a state of mind in which these loyalties took on reality. In some way, it teased the thought of village men and women beyond village boundaries and the Here and Now of their lives. It stood for the eternal against the transient."

Let a man worship in Spirit *and* in truth, as we discussed in earlier chapters, and he will find his mind being teased, little by little, beyond village boundaries; lured from the here and now toward things eternal. The person who begins to lift his eyes from the ground to the hills will learn that his strength comes from God; and thus will deal a formidable blow to the prison gates where multitudes live and die.

Our last view of hell is seen in a life with no destination beyond the grave. The devil has no fear of a church that focuses exclusively on this life. The bigger the church—the busier, the more efficient—the better Satan likes it.

In this, he is smarter than the average church member. "Let's not worry about heaven," that person might say. "We've got no time for pie-in-the-sky religion, or the obscurantism of otherworldliness that fails to see God at work in the very fabric of life in which all of humanity is woven."

It all sounds very modern, enlightened, emancipated.

But the devil knows better. He knows that a Church persuaded of its eternal destiny, and the eternal life of all the souls in it, is a dangerous threat to have loosed on the world. People who claim citizenship in the colony of heaven regard their own lives as expendable for righteousness' sake. Even death is swallowed up for people who form an indestructible communion with Christ. They shine like stars in a dark world, and no darkness can put out their light. The source of their light is Jesus, who "loved the church and gave himself for her" (Ephesians 5:25).

Many of the covenants of the early New England churches ended with the phrase "as befits those whom God has bound together in a little bundle of eternal life." It is a paradox beyond the grasp of the wisdom of this world that those whom God has bound into a little bundle of eternal life are fearsome adversaries for every evil contained in this world.

But let's ask ourselves a question, the same question we asked near the beginning of this chapter: have we drawn too rosy a picture of the Church? does the part of the Church we know fit it?

It is true that individual churches have often chosen, tragically, to specialize in irrelevancies. Churches can represent simply the religious arm of the country club, the Chamber of Commerce, or a political party at prayer.

Twentieth-Century poet Stephen Spender's terrible indictment has been justified: "Religion stands, the Church blocking the sun." The Church stands accused. It pleads guilty, faces its critics without excuse.

But the Church at its best is a Church that is repentant, on its knees seeking and receiving forgiveness, being renewed daily by the mighty power of the Holy Spirit continually at work. Somewhere at its heart is the One who still promises that where two or three are gathered in His name, He will be there.

So, despite its flaws, the Church is still a little kingdom of love, an island in the sea of evil, joined by invisible bonds to a greater Kingdom beyond the horizon—a sight to make hell tremble.

In the third century, St. Cyprian, who became Bishop of Carthage and was later martyred for his faith, wrote to a friend some words powerful enough to terrorize all of hell. Listen to his words:

> "This seems a cheerful world, Donatus, when I view it from this fair garden, under the shadow of these vines. But if I climbed to some great mountain and looked out over the wide lands, you know very well what I would see: brigands on the high roads; pirates on the seas; in the amphitheatres men murdered to please the applauding crowds; under all roofs misery and selfishness. It is really a bad world, Donatus, an

incredibly bad world. Yet, in the midst of it, I have found a quiet and holy people. They have discovered a joy which is a thousand times better than any pleasure of this sinful life. They are despised and persecuted, but they care not. They have overcome the world. These people, Donatus, are the Christians, and I am one of them."

XI

Life on Wings

"Hast thou not known? Hast thou not heard, that the everlasting God, the Lord, the Creator of the ends of the earth, fainteth not, neither is weary? There is no searching of his understanding.

He giveth power to the faint; and to them that have no might he increaseth strength. Even the youths shall faint and be weary, and the young men shall utterly fall:

But they that wait upon the Lord shall renew their strength; they shall mount up with wings as eagles; they shall run, and not be weary; and they shall walk, and not faint" (Isaiah 40: 28-31).

When I was a child, our family moved to a place near a valley in Vermont called Eagle Hollow. I used to love to sit in that hollow, surrounded by steep cliffs on either side, and watch for the golden eagles that could be seen there. I was fascinated, and developed an interest early in these magnificent birds.

More recently—specifically for the last seven years—I have left my home in Darien, Connecticut, and taken a shuttle flight to Washington, D.C., every Monday morning in order to teach a large Bible class. And every Monday morning I have breakfast at Washington's National Airport in a restaurant called The Golden Eagle.

The decor of this restaurant is based on all kinds of eagles that one finds in the United States.

I am a voracious reader by nature, and over the years I have read, with cereal-box fervency, the descriptions of these eagles again and again. Thus, during my seven years of breakfasting at National Airport, I have become something of an authority on eagles!

So it is with special enthusiasm that I approach the thirtieth chapter of Proverbs in which the author makes a strange confession. He admits there are three things beyond his ability to understand. Then he corrects himself. No, he says, there are four:

> "The way of an eagle in the air; the way of a serpent upon a rock; the way of a ship in the midst of the sea; and the way of a man with a maid" (Proverbs 30:19).

A group of Christian scholars in the Second Century, attempting to find all kinds of mystic meanings in obscure passages of the Scripture, claimed that these four mysteries from Proverbs actually represent four great mysteries of the faith.

The way of a man with a maid, they said, speaks of the mystery of Christ's relationship to the Church. The way of a ship in the midst of the sea speaks of the mystery of God's preservation of His people down through the centuries. The way of a serpent upon a rock speaks of Jesus' victory over Satan. And the way of an eagle in the air speaks of the kind of life you and I are called to live by the power of the Holy Spirit.

The more I think about it, the more I think those early Christians may have had something. So in this chapter, I want to look at the way of an eagle in the air, and appeal, not only to our understanding, but also to our imagination, that we might grasp some wonderful truths about Christian life.

The first point I want to make, though, will seem terribly obvious: if you're ever to grow up to be an eagle, you've got to first be born an eagle.

Now that seems apparent when we talk about eagles. (Crows and canaries, for example, will never become eagles!) But it is just as true when we talk about Christians. If you're ever to grow up to be a Christian, somewhere along the line you've got to be born again as a Christian.

We have already discussed the necessity of conversion (or "turning about"). We have looked at the conversation Jesus had with Nicodemus, recorded in John 3, in which Jesus told him he needed to be born again. We have seen that natural life—the kind of life you and I derive from our parents—can produce only natural life and that it requires the Holy Spirit to produce the life of God within us.

So becoming a Christian is like starting life all over again. We need to have the life of God planted within us through the action of the Holy Spirit. To grow up to be an eagle, we must have been born as an eagle.

My second point about eagles is a most wonderful thing! It has to do with the way a mother eagle constructs her nest and rears her young.

She usually builds her nest on the face of a cliff, never completely at the top lest the nest be violated. The Bible knows all about this, of course. "Is it at your command," God asks Job, "that the eagle mounts up and makes his nest on high? On the rock he dwells and makes his home in the fastness of the rocky crag" (Job 39:27-28).

The eagle's nest, moreover, is made with great and consummate skill. It is large, constructed of branches intertwined so as to make it very strong. Finally, the nest is lined with feathers and grass to make it soft.

Once the eggs have been laid and hatched, it becomes the mother eagle's seemingly endless task of going out, getting the food and bringing it back to the baby birds. This she does over and over and over. Each time she returns, she perches on the edge of the nest and feeds the eaglets one by one.

People who study this kind of thing have discovered that you can rearrange the order of the little birds while the mother is gone, yet she still knows exactly which ones have been fed and sees to it that all her babies are nourished equally.

But one day when she comes back, she doesn't rest on the side of the nest and she has nothing in her mouth. This time she flies in and hovers almost motionless in mid-air about three feet above the nest. (I don't know whether you knew an eagle could do that. It can do what a hummingbird can do and remain almost stationary, moving its wings gently.)

I am sure, if little eagles could talk, that one would turn to the others and say, "My, what strong wings Mommy has!"

That's just the point. The mother eagle must now teach her little ones that they are destined to fly, and that those curious appendages on their backs actually have some useful function.

So on this particular day, after hovering overhead, the mother eagle descends into the nest, snuggles up against her little ones with her great head beside them and begins to move them ever so slightly toward the edge of the nest. She continues to nudge, and nudge, and nudge, until—

"Mother, you wouldn't!"

But she does. She casts her eaglets out of the nest, and those little birds go hurtling down the face of the cliff, surely to their destruction.

But not so, because quick as a flash the mother eagle swoops down and catches them on her back and bears them up and puts them back into the nest. And she repeats this process again and again.

Now why would a mother eagle want to do a thing like this? Is it that she no longer loves these little birds?

Not at all! It's because these birds were made to fly, but they don't know it yet. And they never will as long as they stay where it's safe and secure. So she casts them out of the nest.

On another day some time later, when that mother eagle returns to her young, she stands on the edge of the nest and begins to pull out the feathers and leaves. She takes the sticks in her strong beak and snaps them in two, and begins to dismantle the nest.

"Mommy, what are you doing?" the little eagles might cry out.

But she pays no attention, and continues to pull the nest apart. As long as the little birds stay in the nest, you see, they will never fly.

Now why have we talked about these ways of the eagle? Because the Bible uses them to teach us about our God. Read this verse from the Old Testament:

> "Like an eagle that stirs up its nest, that flutters over its young, spreading out its wings, catching them, bearing them on its pinions, the Lord alone did lead him..." (Deuteronomy 32:11-12).

Have you noticed that we can learn something from the way of an eagle in the air? Sometimes our God takes our lives and "casts us out" of all the securities about us.

Have you ever known that feeling? Have you ever had life together just as you wanted it, but then everything seemed to fall apart? Have you ever felt that you'd been removed from your securities and all those things you had counted on?

God is at work in your life; and at those times He may have been pushing you out of the nest.

Now why would He do a thing like that? Is it because He no longer loves you?

Not at all! It's because you and I were made to fly. We were not made to grovel in the dust of the earth; we were made to soar in the heights. So God begins to deal with all the little securities we've built around ourselves, just so He might teach us His immense power.

There is something else about eagles that is most wonderful. Did I say a moment ago that they fly? Oh no, eagles do not fly. Other birds fly, if by "fly" you mean move through the air flapping their wings furiously.

An eagle does not do that. It seems to have an instinctive way of discerning air currents. It also has the ability to lock its wings and wait for the right breeze. When the right breeze comes along, the eagle simply lets go and rides the wind.

Do you know that in the Old Testament, the Hebrew word for wind, *ruach,* is the very same as the word for Spirit? The equivalent Greek word in the New Testament, *pneuma,* is also translated both wind and Spirit.

Eagle Christians, then, are people prepared to fly. But they don't move until they catch the wind of God's Spirit—and then they are borne aloft.

God's work, you see, cannot be accomplished by human might and ingenuity. The Christian life cannot be lived victoriously by our own effort. It is a life to be lived borne aloft by the power of God's Spirit.

"They who wait for the Lord shall renew their strength, they shall mount up with wings like eagles, they shall run and not be weary, they shall walk and not faint" (Isaiah 40:31).

There is a fourth fascinating characteristic of eagles: they seem to possess an innate sense of their own approaching death. If you were to visit the Smithsonian Institution in Washington, D.C., and look at the eagle exhibit, you would learn all about this.

When an eagle has a premonition of death, it leaves its nest and flies to a rock. It fastens its talons to the edge of the rock and looks straight into the setting sun. Then it dies.

I saw an eagle die once. He was my father, and he was almost the same age that I am today. He had a great many talents and gifts, and I loved him.

He was never sick until that last summer. I had just graduated from high school, and he asked me if I would drive for him, since his business took him on many trips. I was happy to do it—partly because I had just gotten my license, but also because it gave me time to be with him.

It was one of my happiest summers as a young man. We drove together for hundreds of miles, my father and I, and talked of many things. It was a wonderful time.

So I will never forget that Sunday in September when we all came downstairs dressed for church. My father was sitting in a large chair in the living room, and he said to us, "I don't feel well enough to go to church today. You all go. I think I'll stay home."

I couldn't believe it! Never in my life had I known my father not to go to church. Although I was born into a traveling family, and we traveled all over the country, always before going to our lodging on a Saturday night we selected a church for the following day. We noted the time of services and how to get there, so that we could worship there the next morning.

So it came as a great shock to me, that Sunday in September, to leave my father behind while we went to church. When we came home, he was sitting in the same chair.

"You know, I'm really not feeling well," he told us. "I think I'd better go into the hospital."

So we made arrangements with the doctor, and had him admitted that very afternoon.

Within a week we were told he had cancer of the bone in a very advanced degree. Within another week he was dead.

I will never forget the last hours we spent with him in his hospital room, because we as his family kept a kind of vigil. We knew it wasn't going to be long.

I remember well the scene: there were my mother, and my father's mother, and his brother and sister, and my brother and sister and I. We were all gathered around him.

A few hours before he died, he lapsed into a coma. Someone there commented that a person in a coma can sometimes hear, though he cannot speak. I didn't know if that was true, but the members of my family left the room and continued their conversation in the hallway while I remained behind.

Before long, however, my father opened his eyes, sat up, and began to talk to me in a perfectly normal way. Quickly I called the rest of the family.

So there we were, gathered around his bed, as my father spoke to each of us in turn.

"Mary," he said, addressing my mother, "we have had thirty-two wonderful years"; and he recapped some of the experiences they had shared over those years.

Then he turned to my older sister, Virginia, and shared some very personal words with her. Then my brother,

Rex. Finally he turned to me. Each of us was addressed in a tender way, about things that had been particularly important in our relationship with him over the years.

When he turned to Grandmother, he said, "Mom, I want you to know I appreciate all you did for me. I know it wasn't easy after Dad's death, but I thank you for it."

And he spoke some words to his brother and sister.

By that time, tears were coursing down our cheeks.

"You know, I understand how you feel," he said. "But if you could hear what I can hear . . . . Do you hear the music? If you could see what I can see, you would not even want me to recover."

Then he seemed to muster all the strength of his weakened body, sat up in bed, and exclaimed, "Rejoice with me! For this is my coronation day!"

With those words, he lay back and died.

Listen, I have seen an eagle die. His feet were planted firmly on the rock, Christ Jesus, his eyes looking straight ahead into the Son of Righteousness.

You know, I'm sure heaven has many wonderful surprises—but I can't believe it held any for my father. He had known the Lord for years, and he moved, at death, right into His nearer presence. There wasn't a trace of fear in him at all. It was all glory as he passed into the presence of his God.

I know that death is a mystery. Sometimes death comes suddenly, sometimes after a long debilitating illness. But I dare to believe there is a difference between a Christian who dies and one who dies without hope.

I believe we can learn something from the eagle: we can stand on the rock, Christ Jesus, fix our eyes on the Son of Righteousness, and, when our time comes, move into the presence of the Lord with great joy.

So there you have it—the way of an eagle in the air. What do we learn?

We learn that if we are ever going to grow up to be a Christian, we have got to be born one. We learn that there are times in life when everything seems to fall apart—God seems to be removing all that is around us—but only because He wants to teach us to fly.

Fly? No, not fly—*soar*. An eagle mounts up and rides the winds; and so are we to move at the impulse of the Spirit of God guiding, providing, leading, directing.

Then, when it is time to die, we can pass into the presence of the Lord God without a trace of fear, translated into glory that we may be with Jesus forevermore.

Let us learn the way of an eagle in the air.

Father, we thank You for Your natural creation. We thank You for the eagle. And we ask that, as we ponder the way of an eagle in the air, we may learn something important about Your truth, and grow in it, to the glory of Your name. Amen.

XII

If I Were The Devil

"Then was Jesus led up of the Spirit into the wilderness to be tempted of the devil.

And when he had fasted forty days and forty nights, he was afterward an hungered.

And when the tempter came to him, he said, If thou be the Son of God, command that these stones be made bread.

But he answered and said, It is written, Man shall not live by bread alone, but by every word that proceedeth out of the mouth of God.

Then the devil taketh him up into the holy city, and setteth him on a pinnacle of the temple,

And saith unto him, If thou be the Son of God, cast thyself down: for it is written, He shall give his angels charge concerning thee: and in their hands they shall bear thee up, lest at any time thou dash thy foot against a stone.

Jesus said unto him, It is written again, Thou shall not tempt the Lord thy God.

Again, the devil taketh him up into an exceeding high

> *mountain, and sheweth him all the kingdoms of the world,*
> *and the glory of them;*
>
> *And saith unto him, All these things will I give thee, if*
> *thou wilt fall down and worship me.*
>
> *Then saith Jesus unto him, Get thee hence, Satan: for it is*
> *written, Thou shalt worship the Lord thy God, and him*
> *only shalt thou serve"*   *(Matthew 4: 1-10).*

If I were the devil (and let me hasten to add, lest there be any question in your mind, that I am not), I would take great pride in what I had accomplished in this world of men and things.

By almost any standard of judgment, my work would have to be considered an unqualified success. Kingdoms and nations have fallen to me; and I have wrought more havoc among men than a thousand IBM machines could possibly compute.

Nearly 2000 years ago, St. John, the beloved disciple of my archenemy, Jesus Christ, spoke of me as "that ancient serpent, who is called the Devil and Satan, the deceiver of the whole world" (Revelation 12:9). And I think you'll agree I have lived up to my reputation.

Sometimes when I think of the cleverness of my deceptions, I am nearly overcome with laughter. Don't you admire my cunning in having deceived almost a whole world as to my person as well as my whereabouts?

Almost everyone thinks of me, for example, as a cute little fellow dressed in a red suit, with horns, tail and a pitchfork. There is something quaint and charming in that, don't you agree? So long as people think of me like that, who would ever suspect that I am the mortal enemy of their souls, out to ruin their lives in this world and the next?

You will never find me wallowing in the gutter and making a fool of myself—not in this world. You will never see me as a jailbird or a dope addict or a whoremonger. You'll never find me robbing banks or burning houses. The world is full of twisted people who can manage all these things for me quite nicely.

No, I prefer to change myself into someone respectable. I can be a gentleman—a nice guy.

It is true that St. Paul saw through this strategy a long time ago when he wrote, "Satan disguises himself as an angel of light" (II Corinthians 11:14). But then, a lot of people don't read St. Paul's writings. I would keep everyone from reading his writings if I could. He's dangerous to my cause; he knew too much.

Paul commented once that Christians were not ignorant of my devices (II Corinthians 2:11). He knew and understood the threat I pose for the Kingdom of God, so he wrote about me in every one of his letters (except that little one to Philemon).

Then, too, my deception has been almost 100 percent effective in regard to my whereabouts. Most people think I spend all my time in booze joints and brothels and gambling parlors.

I almost never go to those places! I let fallen human nature take care of my business there. I prefer to work behind the scenes in places where I'm not expected.

Since many of you reading this are church people, I'll let you in on some of my plans for dealing with professed Christians (although I'm at work in many other places and among many other people).

One of my brightest strategies is making people think I am unalterably opposed to churches and religion.

Nothing could be further from the truth! Some of the most effective agencies I have for accomplishing my purposes are churches with just enough religion to inoculate their members against anything really significant, so far as the Christian faith is concerned.

St. Paul hit it right on the head (oh, there I go

mentioning his name again, but I can hardly help it, so well did he have me figured out), when he warned young Timothy about churches "holding the form of religion but denying the power of it" (II Timothy 3:5).

From my point of view, a little religion is a good thing. It gives people a warm glow inside. It tends to confirm their complacency.

Some people attend church because it's the social thing to do; others because they've always done it, or because it's good for business. Or you meet the "right" sort of people there. These are all marvelous reasons, of which I wholly approve!

Another delightful thing is, many ministers and priests (you'd be surprised if you knew how many), wouldn't dream of disturbing people's complacency. Some of them know that the Gospel of Jesus Christ confronts men and women with their need and God's solution—but they also know that a lot of people don't want to hear this.

I have convinced many other ministers and priests that the Gospel of Jesus Christ just isn't relevant anymore. These folks exchange the Gospel willingly for the latest gimmick. "We must make Christ relevant," you hear them say (as if Christ were not as relevant today as He was 2000 years ago!).

My primary attack on the Church, however, it not a frontal attack. I tried that once with Jesus in the wilderness and came away thoroughly trounced.

No, I like to attack in other ways. I engage in espionage; I act as a fifth columnist, working from within to undermine a church's ministry.

I try to get as many people as possible to believe that I don't exist—especially clergymen. (I give a lot of personal attention to clergymen, for I've discovered that if I can capture the pulpit of a church, most of the pews will also fall to me without much trouble.)

But since I cannot persuade everyone that I don't exist, I

sometimes try the opposite tack: I get certain people to "over-believe." I make them think I'm invincible.

There is nothing so effective in breaking down a human's defenses as a good stiff case of defeatism! If I can get a person to throw up his hands at all the corruption in politics, and all the evil in the world, and make him think there is not a thing he can do about it, then I've hooked him for sure.

Another part of my program for the Church is deflecting it as early as possible from its most important task: fulfilling Jesus' command to go into all the world and preach the Gospel to every creature. It doesn't matter what they do, as long as they fail to do that!

I also encourage them to put great confidence in human organizations and very little in the power of God. I like them to think they can bring about God's Kingdom by their own efforts; that the success of God's work depends upon their ŏwn skills and talents and ingenuity.

I have tried to bury, or to discredit as fanatical, the words of that ancient prophet of Israel, who said God's work is accomplished "not by might, nor by power, but by my Spirit, says the Lord of hosts" (Zechariah 4:6).

Another of my strategies is keeping clergymen and church people from developing a balanced view of Christian mission.

I get some Christians to believe Christianity is concerned only with heaven and the next life, and I make them obnoxious in their attempt to save souls. I get other Christians to believe Christianity has to do only with reconciling man with man, and righting social ills.

You would think it would dawn on some of them that Christianity has both a horizontal and a vertical dimension—that it restores relationships among humans and also with God through faith in Jesus Christ. (The Scripture is absolutely clear about both dimensions, but I have been marvelously successful in keeping people from reading and studying their Bibles!)

One of my most noteworthy campaigns has been in making people believe that the great words of the Christian faith—sin, salvation, regeneration, redemption—are no longer meaningful. They are "fuddy-duddy," old-fashioned. I've even gotten some clergymen to say they don't believe in sin anymore!

I've accomplished this by causing the majority of people to lose all sense of righteousness and holiness of God. I get people to think of God as a doting old grandfather who indulges His people in their little indiscretions.

If people live in the dark long enough, you see, and never come to the light and look into the mirror, they can have dirt on their faces and never know it. So long as I can get people to compare themselves only with their friends and neighbors, I've accomplished my purpose. (Compared with some people, after all, anybody would look righteous!)

But when people begin to move toward God, and when they begin to understand God's Word and the demands for holiness that He places upon them, then they begin to see themselves as God sees them. When this happens, they see their need before God, and come to Christ as their Savior.

I can still hear the words of Christ thundering down the corridors of time: "You shall love the Lord your God with all your heart, and with all your soul, and with all your mind. This is the great and first commandment. And a second is like it, You shall love your neighbor as yourself" (Matthew 22:37-39).

If a person understands what these words mean, the only possible response he can make is, "Lord have mercy upon me, Christ have mercy upon me."

Now look at me! Here I am talking about the Gospel as though I were a Christian preacher. I understand the Gospel as well as any Christian preacher, of course—and better than many—but the fact is, it is my job to prevent people on earth, both inside and outside of the Church, from understanding it. I think I do a pretty good job, don't you?

Sometimes I have to develop an alternative plan of attack if my first plan doesn't work very well. So if I can't get people to give up every connection with the church, then I try to get them all hung up on inconsequential matters. I call it majoring on the minors.

I push for more dialogue, more buzz sessions, endless discussion on unimportant points. I try to get people more interested in antichrist than in Jesus Christ; more concerned about where Cain got his wife than about how they treat their own wives; more involved in condemning someone else's experience than in personally being filled with the Holy Spirit.

Oh yes, while we are on the subject of the Holy Spirit, let me tell you what I have done here. I have tried to confuse interest in the Holy Spirit with emotionalism. I have been tremendously successful in arousing people's suspicions whenever emotion is linked with the Christian faith.

I let people feel deeply in other areas, of course, and become emotionally involved in movies, television programs, books and sports of all kinds. At the same time, I prompt the idea—inconsistent though it is—that to feel deeply about God is fanaticism.

One way or another, I use emotion—or the lack of it—to keep people away from the Lord God.

I could go on and on, detailing my many strategies for enticing as much of the human race as possible into hell. But I trust I have said enough for you to be impressed with the cleverness of my schemes, and to realize that I have amply lived up to my job description as the deceiver of the whole world.

Now if I were the devil, as I wrote at the beginning of this chapter, those are some of the things I would do.

But, as I said before, I am not the devil. As a matter of fact, at one point in my life, I promised to renounce the devil and all his works, the vain pomp and glory of the world with all its covetous desires, the sinful desires of the flesh, and I determined, with the help of God, not to follow nor be led by them.

The Scripture depicts the Christian's struggle with evil as a battle. At the end of St. Paul's letter to the Ephesians, for example, he writes of this warfare in these words:

> "Finally, be strong in the Lord and in the strength of his might. Put on the whole armor of God, that you may be able to stand against the wiles of the devil.... Stand therefore, having girded your loins with truth, and having put on the breastplate of righteousness, and having shod your feet with the equipment of the gospel of peace; above all taking the shield of faith, with which you can quench all the flaming darts of the evil one. And take the helmet of salvation, and the sword of the Spirit, which is the word of God" (Ephesians 6:10-11, 14-17).

Let me point out three things about the Christian's equipment to do battle with the devil.

First, notice that, with all the pieces of armor listed, nothing protects the back of the Christian soldier. This suggests to me that God wants us to confront the forces of evil head-on, as it were. We are not to turn around in retreat.

Second, notice that all the pieces of armor save one are for defense. The girdle of truth, the breastplate of righteousness, the shoes of the Gospel of peace, the shield of faith, the helmet of salvation—all these defend the Christian from attacks from without.

Third, there is only one piece of equipment given to us in launching an offensive against the enemy, and that is the sword of the Spirit—the Word of God. God has given us His own Word, the holy Scriptures, as our most powerful weapon to destroy the works of the devil.

Do you remember Jesus' encounter with Satan as recorded in Matthew 4? There came, first, the temptation to turn stones into bread. What was Jesus' reply? "It is written, 'Man shall not live by bread alone, but by every word that proceeds from the mouth of God'" (verse 4).

In the second temptation, high on the pinnacle of the Temple, the devil urged Jesus to cast Himself down, reminding Him that the angels would bear Him up. But Jesus responded, "Again, it is written, 'You shall not tempt the Lord your God'" (verse 7).

In the third temptation, the devil promised Jesus all the kingdoms of the world, if only He would fall down and worship him. Jesus replied, "It is written, 'You shall worship the Lord your God, and him only shall you serve'" (verse 10).

In each instance, Jesus responded with the words, "It is written."

I am not suggesting for a minute that all you have to do to defeat the devil is quote a few verses of Scripture. Not at all.

But I want to state as clearly as possible that a life built on the Word of God is built on a sure foundation. When the truth of God is woven into the very fabric of our lives, we are in a position to understand the will of God and to expose the works of darkness.

The psalmist wrote:

"How can a young man keep his way pure? By

guarding it according to thy word ... Thy word is
a lamp to my feet and a light to my path" (Psalm
119:9, 105).

The writer to the Hebrews declared:

"The word of God is living and active, sharper
than any two-edged sword, piercing to the
division of soul and spirit, of joints and marrow,
and discerning the thoughts and intentions of
the heart" (Hebrews 4:12).

Let me encourage you to become thoroughly familiar
with the use of this mighty weapon God has provided for
spiritual warfare. For it is by skillful handling of the sword
of the Spirit, the Word of God, that you and I will be able to
join with our Lord, Jesus Christ, who came "to destroy the
works of the devil" (I John 3:8).

Be swift to hear the Word of God and bind it to your
hearts. Be strong in the power of His might. And I can
promise you that the battle will be ours.

For those of you utilizing the tapes, we thank you for joining us on the Episcopal Series of the Protestant Hour and we ask that God's rich blessing may be with each one of you this day and always. Amen.